WEALTH
— *On* —
PURPOSE®

A Field Guide for
New Business Owners

CARLOS H. LOWENBERG, JR., ChFC®

Published by Advantage, Charleston, South Carolina.
Member of Advantage Media Group.

ADVANTAGE is a registered trademark and the Advantage colophon is a trademark of Advantage Media Group, Inc.

Printed in the United States of America.

ISBN: 978-1-59932-705-1
LCCN: 2016944065

Cover design by Matt Morse.

This publication is designed to provide accurate and authoritative information in regard to the subject matter covered. It is sold with the understanding that the publisher is not engaged in rendering legal, accounting, or other professional services. If legal advice or other expert assistance is required, the services of a competent professional person should be sought.

Lowenberg Group LLC, dba Lowenberg Wealth Management Group (LWMG), is a registered investment advisor. Advisory services are only offered to clients or prospective clients where Lowenberg Group LLC, and its representatives are properly licensed or exempt from licensure. No advice may be rendered by Lowenberg Group LLC, unless a client service agreement is in place.

The opinions expressed in this book are for general informational purposes only and are not intended to provide specific advice or recommendations for any individual or on any specific security. It is only intended to provide education about the financial industry and should not be regarded as a description of advisory services provided by Lowenberg Group, LLC. Any mention of a particular security and related performance data is not a recommendation to buy or sell that security. Lowenberg Group, LLC manages its clients' accounts using a variety of investment techniques and strategies, which are not necessarily discussed in this book. Investments in securities involve the risk of loss. Any past performance discussed during this book is no guarantee of future results. Any indices referenced for comparison are unmanaged and cannot be invested into directly. To determine which investments may be appropriate for you, consult your financial advisor prior to investing. As always, please remember, investing involves risk and possible loss of principal capital; please seek advice from a licensed professional.

— DEDICATION —

To Nicole, I thought this up in many of our conversations over the years. And to my clients, especially a few who have passed on: Martin Blank and Ken and Martha Langham. Their constant encouragement, challenge, and leadership inspired me. Until we meet again.

— Acknowledgements —

I would like to acknowledge, first and foremost, my writing assistant, project manager, and proofreader, Julie Rompel. Who doesn't go by any of those titles by the way, and in her day job is our operations manager. Her indefatigable and constant attention to this project made it possible.

I would also like to acknowledge Georgia Kirke for helping me get my thoughts on paper.

— CONTENTS —

— INTRODUCTION —

I watched, engrossed, as Rocky punched it out with Apollo Creed up on the big screen one afternoon when my father took me to a matinee in El Paso. I was eleven years old, but even at that age, I knew something about boxing. Dad was a fan of the sport. We had visited gyms, and he had even taken me to fights.

"Son, do you know what the lesson of that movie was?" My dad asked when we walked out of the theatre. I remember feeling, "what did I miss?" Rocky had lost. It was a real slugfest. I knew that he did his best and that he really shouldn't have had a chance. This was the first time I remember thinking that the good guy didn't win! But I couldn't for the life of me think of what my dad was looking for. "I don't know, Dad." I really wanted to know, and I really wanted to have the right answer. I thought about it more and finally toward the end of the drive home, my dad said, "If you work hard enough and you have enough time, you can accomplish anything you want."

Perhaps you remember being told something similar by a parent or grandparent when you were young? How many times throughout your career do memories like these filter through into the present, usually just when you're wondering what the next step is, challenging the direction you are going in and trying to make decisions that ensure you are always on your own path rather than drifting into somebody else's?

This advice has certainly stayed with me ever since that day at that movie, like when I embarked on a college degree thinking I was destined to become an accounting and finance major, only to discover my real interest was philosophy, so I majored in that instead. Or like during the 1987 depression in Texas when I decided that learning how to sell would be a great foundation for my career, only to discover that companies weren't necessarily looking to buy company benefits in a recession. Or when I eventually decided to combine my love of people and ideas with consultative selling, observing the real dangers people were facing and the depth of their concerns.

I fought for victory in those early days of my career, and I was determined, with Rocky Balboa a sort of role model, to come back fighting in each round and never give up. I knew that with time and perseverance, Austin would rise again and that I, too, would be all right. I knew I had a bright future ahead of me, even if I couldn't see it yet, because I knew that if I wanted something badly enough, and if I kept at it, I could do anything.

—— FORWARD WITH CONfiDENCE ——

The power of great advice like my father's, I've come to learn, does not come from simply hearing it. It comes from the act of embedding it into your mind-set, and using it to inform your every day decision-making. You have to live it and make it a habit before you can reap the rewards.

Having worked with hundreds of successful business leaders from all types of backgrounds, one thing I've observed is that most, like me, fight for their successes. They choose themselves and their own path in life and in doing so, they often find themselves in the position of pioneer, constantly venturing down the unbeaten track while leading the way for others to follow. It's what makes us "entrepreneurial," and our ability to create our futures by using our individual strengths to create value for others will always provide for us in one way or another.

The flip side to this entrepreneurial nature, however, is that the "right" way forward is not always clear. There are plenty of crossroads and forks, hazards and distractions en route to our bigger futures, and particularly in our rapidly changing economic and technological landscape, it can be hard to identify long-term goals and create a plan for our businesses and our wealth that we have true confidence in. It can also be hard to know how to think about your business and your wealth. I deal with this every single day in my own business, helping successful business leaders build and manage their wealth and indeed, their legacies, through a combination of careful planning and cultivating the right mind-set.

The purpose of this book is to provide the leadership, clarity, and confidence to help you make informed decisions about your business wealth, your personal wealth, and your and your family's futures. Written specifically for entrepreneurs and small business owners who want to be sure that they are working on those things that can have the most impact, this book serves as a guide that aims to improve your understanding of working on, versus in, your business, and to introduce many of you to new ways of thinking about wealth creation and thus help you get more of what you want in life and less of what you don't. Over the course of the next two hours, I will share my experience and expertise to show you how you can create the future you want and take your business to the next level, without adding a lot of risk. Everything I share in this book comes from my experience working with closely held businesses and their owners.

—— GREAT LEADERSHIP ——

Leadership can be defined in many ways, but great leadership certainly involves changing one's situation for the better. Which way should you go? What should you do? I work with business owners to develop a trusting relationship in which we can answer those questions. When you have leadership from a service provider, you not only have the confidence that they know what they are doing, and can therefore be trusted, but you are also empowered to start making better decisions for yourself. Leadership is, therefore, a mind-set, a practice, that can be both provided by others and generated from within and, when you have it, you can move forward toward your goals confidently, minimizing the risks as you go.

People often think of business owners as big risk takers. Instead, they are risk mitigators. Successful business owners eliminate as many risks as they can, getting those obstacles out of their way as they achieve their goals. They do so through planning, and planning requires a degree of clarity.

For years I have run my own business, and I understand the ups and downs. Along the way, I also have worked with hundreds of business owners as they have faced a wide variety of scenarios, through markets good and bad, through bleak economies, and through internal challenges. I have dealt with both routine matters and unusual and intense issues. Once, for example, as I arrived for a meeting with a CEO, two police cruisers pulled in behind me.

The company's controller had been embezzling. I'd say that's an issue, as did the business. One minute everything was fine and the next, chaos.

In one form or another for twenty-five years, I have been working with business owners. In my early Austin days, I would give those sales presentations and listen as the owners informed me why what I was suggesting was wrong. I often went back to my office convinced that they knew a lot more than I did, which of course was true. But I listened. I took it in, and I took it to heart. I learned. And in the many years and many conversations since, I have continued to build my breadth of knowledge and understanding. I have seen the patterns and come up with solutions, and I'm pleased to share them throughout this book.

—— THE BUSINESS LIFE CYCLE ——

Every business has a life cycle, but it's easiest to visualize it as an S-curve given business will be in some stage of that life cycle. It might be the early stage of survival, or the period of growth, or the later time of maturity or disinvestment, when the company is at the point of selling or transitioning.

START UP & SURVIVAL	GROWTH	MATURITY	TRANSITION
FOCUS	FOCUS	FOCUS	FOCUS
Cash Flow	Cash Flow	Expense and Tax Reduction	
Increasing Capacity	Key Employee Group		Owner Divest
Marketing	Contingency Plans		Tax Avoidance at Sale/Transfer
Financial Systems	Financial Controls	Key Person Retention	Lifetime Financial Confidence
Right People		Value Driver Exit Strategies	
		Owner Financial and Estate Planning	Target Succession

When in the growth stage, businesses attach greater importance to matters that they did not pay much attention to in the survival stage. In the maturity stage, businesses move on to other pressing concerns that had yet to present themselves in the growth stage. And at the point of selling or passing the company on to the next generation, still other matters take on prime importance.

No matter what stage of your business you are in right now, this book shares information and recommended actions that will add to your knowledge of what is important in all those stages, and how to make the most of them. Having worked with owners at all levels for over twenty years, I understand the opportunities and challenges both from the psychological and financial perspectives. I know how it feels to be where you are, and I know what needs to be put in place to get to the next level.

Two things are of highest concern in the growth stage. The company needs to make sure that its financing is in place, whether self-financing or from the outside. And it needs to make sure that it is building a stable and motivated management team to get to maturity. In the mature stage, the focus is on making sure that the business supports the owner, who also needs to keep a perspective on what is most important. Often the owner can get distracted when the business is mature, or seems to be, and is making lots of money. This book will not tell you how to manage your business, but it does show what becomes very important as the business grows beyond the survival stage including how to build and nurture your team, and work with your end goals in mind.

—— WALKING ON THE MOON

Business owners often say that they sometimes feel as if they are walking on the moon. They feel like they are the only ones to know what they are going through, to do what they have done. Not too many of their friends and associates have also built $50 million or $100 million businesses. Or, if anyone has, the business is in an entirely different field. Even though the principles tend to be the same regardless of the nature of the enterprise, many business owners do not necessarily see it that way.

It is common for a business owner to see themselves as different. It can be a lonely life. Throughout this book we will explore the various principles, mind-sets, and resources available to business owners to silence our inner critic. It is possible and accessible no matter how far away that point seems right now, and in learning and then practicing the habits that open you up to receiving wealth and security, you surely will.

With that said, lacking that feeling of connection, business owners may find it difficult to find a trusted advisor to help them grow and this tends to increase the more they do expand and explore new areas. As the business gets more complex, so do the associated issues. Some of those issues are directly related to the business, such as tax and accounting concerns and operational challenges. Some are more personal in nature. Whatever your concerns are, if you've convinced yourself that they're unique to you, then you might also be wondering where on earth you will find a specialist to help you execute your growth plans. If you live and work in a small town, you may feel the situation is hopeless. You understand that you are in need of good counsel, but you want that advice to be practical. You do not want to hear suggestions that do not apply to you, or that even could lead you astray if you were to follow them.

Let me reassure you that business owners of diverse disciplines still have quite a lot in common. They face similar challenges. They tend to feel as if they are paying too much in taxes, for example. They face the same kind of pressures as they work with the same tax code to find ways to pay less. I had one client recently tell me, when referring to one of his key execs and a partner in the firm he owns, that "he is the only one I can tell everything I know and think about the business to."

It can feel lonely up there at the top, and business owners often do find it difficult to connect with a community of people in the same situation. That feeling of isolation is, in itself, something they have in common. They feel that they have to figure it out on their own. It need not be so. There are avenues of good advice available that can bridge the common concerns of a wide array of business owners. You may feel that you are walking on the moon, but in truth there is fertile ground all around.

What business owners who feel like they're in this alone have on their minds often has much to do with where they are in the business cycle. One business might have $70 million and be in growth mode. The CEO is wondering: "How do I safely and securely grow this thing as much as possible?" Another business might be maturing, and its owner is wondering: "How do I keep this growing steadily and make sure that what I have created doesn't end up hurting my family?"

Often those in the latter situation feel more confused than those who are in the former. They may still feel driven to grow and improve the business, but they see what is happening in the families of some of their friends, where the kids seem spoiled from too much affluence. "Why should I keep doing this?" they may wonder—but they do not know what else they might do.

My objective for this book, first and foremost, is to cut through the confusion. If you are in that position, you might want to understand your situation in black and white and to recognize your options for dealing with it. You may feel paralyzed and unable to act because you can't figure out what you truly need and what you should be doing.

"I want to leave everything to charity except enough to my kids so that they will never need anything," a client told me recently.

"Well, how much is that?" I asked. "Would that be $5 million per kid? Would it be $2 million?"

"I don't know."

And because he had not been able to answer that question, he had not moved forward with his attorney in drafting his estate plan.

For most business owners, it's not as if anything is going terribly wrong, but they do have conflicted feelings and so many unanswered questions. Still, they keep at it, pursuing the status quo, encouraged by the fact that they are making several million dollars a year. They may not be certain of the right thing to do, but it appears they are doing something right. Meanwhile, it is easy to feel attacked from all sides. One client described it as a "war on wealth"—whether it's from taxes or increased regulations. On the one hand, colleagues in entrepreneurial groups praise the spirit of innovation. But it can feel as though the government is not on your side; not when the top 1 percent of the taxpayers pay nearly half of the tax. We have recently seen capital gains taxes rising by 50 percent, and income taxes by 25 to 30 percent.

So it can be easy to feel as if prosperity is being taken from you. I have also met people who feel that the government might as well take a big share because the kids would make even more of a mess of it. I have met people who gave too much to their kids too early, and then conditions changed and they did not have enough for themselves. They needed it back. It can be hard to imagine, but people do lose $50 million. They can lose everything. The money can evaporate in a bad economy, or it could evaporate because of a personal catastrophe.

And when people are faced with the big questions, typically their response is to persevere. They work to build their business and eventually sell for what they hope will be a good price. Once they sell, they think they know that the proceeds should go into the market—and they worry about whether they will lose control. Whatever stage you're at, it is important to plan carefully to keep your options open. The key is to remember the why, the purpose, the reason that you are deciding either to part with your money or not. You might give to your kids, or you might give to charity. Or you might even opt to pay the most you can in taxes—and yes, once in a while, someone chooses to pay the maximum tax! With real life examples and thinking exercises, this book goes through each of the scenarios with the aim of eliminating your confusion and providing direction.

—— SOMEONE ON YOUR SIDE ————————————————

The good news is there is so much you can do. There are steps you can take to gain reassurance so that you can move forward with confidence. First you need someone in whom you can feel confident. With professional guidance, you can put in motion your plan for prosperity.

Although we work hard to find the big picture, a lot of times business owners come to us with a very specific issue. We will zero in on the situation that the client needs to deal with immediately. We explain the options. "I didn't know I could do that," I often hear. "Tell me how that works." And then we'll talk about the details of succession planning, or about rewarding key employees as a retention strategy. As we discuss the specifics, sometimes the conversation broadens into larger issues with which we can also be of assistance. We show them what is possible, the solutions that are available with the right kind of planning. We challenge assumptions, such as the attitude that only the very wealthy can reduce their tax bill.

I have often noticed that people can make multimillions and yet do not think of themselves as big fish or particularly sophisticated. It's as if they have a radar that can only see fish that are bigger than themselves. They might be bringing in many millions per year, but what they notice is that others have more. Perceptions of wealth are relative. Rest assured: there are strategies that can help every business person, wherever you are along that S-curve, whatever stage your business is in. You just need to have someone on your side to go through the information with you with structure and clarification.

—— WASTE NOT, WANT NOT ——

Business owners never think of themselves as wasteful, but they do spend a lot of time concerned about matters of efficiency. They can begin to feel frustrated as the money keeps slipping away even as the business grows. The prospect of paying so much in taxes tends to dim the entrepreneurial spirit.

"I feel like I finally got my business where I wanted it to be," one man told me recently, "and it's making good money. But it seems that half of that goes to taxes, and the other half I have to save to make sure the business will be okay. I'm hitting my goals, and the company's five times larger than it was when I bought it—but it just doesn't feel that I'm much further along." It had been his father's business, and he bought it from his mother after his father died. It was doing about $2 million in sales and had grown to about $14 million in sales. But as it has grown, he has been handing over 40 percent of his earnings to the government, and when he passes the business on to his own child, he expects that the government will be taking another 25 percent cut. I reassured him that we can eliminate the second tax completely and cut the first one down, but the frustration he expressed is common among business people. It can feel as if the odds of success are stacked against them. They can feel like saying, "why even try?"

Here's why. A business has the potential of doing tremendous good in the world. It supports not only the owner's family but the families of all employees, not to mention the service it provides for all those customers. That's a worthy cause.

In fact, the government knows that, too—and therefore puts in place tax incentives that businesses can use to reduce how much they must pay. Lower taxation makes businesses more competitive and productive. It frees up your resources so you can grow stronger, better serve your customers and your staff, and ultimately reach out to give back to the community. Clearly that is in the government's interest. The difference is that you, rather than the government, get to decide where the money goes.

Knowing that I can help people find those efficiencies and savings is a reason for me to get up every day. I am more than happy to help them break free of their acceptance of the status quo. I help them to understand that there is much they can do, and they need not feel that it's all stacked against them. I help them to develop those strategies, and I also look for the good things they already are doing that could be made so much better with some judicious adjustments.

First and foremost, a business must grow. It needs to thrive. That's why it is so important to define all the efficiencies and eliminate anything wasteful. This gives it the ability to do good not just in some distant day of charitable giving—although that is important, too—but also in the here and now. Thriving businesses produce the pay checks for countless citizens. Thriving businesses support local efforts and campaigns. They contribute immensely to the economic and social health of a community.

And yet so many businesses that could do even more to help their communities are simply leaving money on the table. They fail to take advantage of strategies that could add significant value to their enterprise. That is why I do what I do and why I've written this book. That is the passion that drives me. I can do my part to improve our community, whether locally or nationally, by helping to put a stop to the waste, one business at a time.

By the end of reading, I hope you feel more informed of these strategies, have a clearly defined purpose and vision for the future and understand the next steps to put this into action.

Part One

— CREATING YOUR VISION —

CHAPTER 1

WEALTH

— *On* —

PURPOSE®

A long-time client of mine operated a construction-related business since the 1970s in Austin's boom-or-bust economy. He went through several of those cycles, emerging stronger and smarter each time. He and his wife lived modestly for a couple with a multimillion-dollar business, and they developed trusting and open relationships with customers, suppliers and staff.

Above all, what they had going for them was a dedication to clear values that drove their decisions. They never lost sight of their top priority, which was to spare their children from the hard lives that they themselves once had known. They also were determined that their business would be highly ethical and reflect their spiritual values. They would do nobody wrong. At times they had skipped their own salaries for months or for a year at a time, but they treated people right and put others first.

The couple was setting money aside so that they could give the business to their children. Because it would not be a sale, they needed enough other resources to carry them through a long life together in retirement. But the founder died far sooner than anyone had imagined, and, as is so often the case, the spouse followed soon after.

The founder had kept his principles intact through the years. Though he was a client, I considered him a mentor. He was not a man of many words, but on occasion we would have deep conversations on the direction and goals of his business and the consequences of his decisions on the company and on the welfare of his staff. He did most of the talking. I listened, and asked probing questions. He was highly introspective and asked good questions of himself. He did what he resolved to do.

I've learned that this is a path to success. You pursue your principles relentlessly. You remind yourself why you got into business in the first place, and you commit to doing right by others. And then you put your hand on the tiller and go after that vision.

—— IN PURSUIT OF PURPOSE ——

Vision is one of those overused words that sounds good when people are trying to prove their point, whatever it might be. "Just find the right vision," 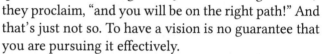 they proclaim, "and you will be on the right path!" And that's just not so. To have a vision is no guarantee that you are pursuing it effectively.

Nonetheless, without a vision for your business you will have nothing to pursue. Good things happen when the vision is clear. You need to develop that clarity—and sometimes a new vision—at each stage of your business' life.

As you get started, you need to be able to see clearly where you are going and why. What will your company look like as it grows and strives? What are you hoping to accomplish? A young person dreaming of starting a business simply might desire the freedom to do things differently than his or her employer requires. That's often where the entrepreneurial spirit is born.

When a business loses its direction and reason for being, its future is bleak. That can happen when money becomes the prime objective, regardless of the ideals and principles upon which the business was built. Profit is a byproduct of doing things right. What happens sometimes, however, is that the profit becomes so attractive that the owner focuses on the money. Doing things right no longer is top of mind. Starved of vision, the business declines.

This poverty of purpose can afflict a business at any of its stages. It can happen as the business is finding its first success, or it can happen as the owner is preparing to transfer it to the children and the family begins focusing on the money and forgetting about the purpose. When the focus is misplaced, it's hard to make good decisions. One bad decision leads to the next in a domino effect that results in a product or service of lower quality.

I have found that the business owners who are my clients are all people of action—and it is their sense of purpose that drives those actions. That is what differentiates them. They ask the good questions and they act on them. They refuse to just float along. Many of them care deeply about the values they will impart to the next generation, and for good reason: if the next generation takes the reins, it is essential that it maintains the founder's intensity of purpose and entrepreneurial spirit. Otherwise, the business will lose its focus and competitive edge.

A symptom of that is the lack of a clear line of leadership. I once sketched out the organizational chart of a company that felt it was having trouble adjusting to changing conditions. The chief operations officer had fifteen direct reports. It should have been no more than three or four. None of them could get sufficient attention. No wonder nothing was getting done.

That's the kind of situation that stops a business in its tracks—and the root of the problem is not always obvious. It happens as a business grows. Two people who were working side by side find themselves, a year or two later, with a level of management between them. That can breed discontent and slow progress to a crawl. So the first step for any growing business looking to create a straightforward and actionable long term plan is to get really clear on the purpose, not just of the business owner but of the organization, too.

—— **SURVIVING THE GROWING PAINS** ——

Several years ago, a business that had survived tough times was beginning to thrive as the economic tide rose. The owner was kicking off quite a surplus of cash. He was doing a lot of things right. He had taken steps, for example, to retain his key people.

But as the cash rolled in, he started investing in areas that created huge liabilities for him when the economy turned back down. One of his investments was in a local development: "This one's a no-brainer!" he declared. I'd like to think there's always a place for brain power in such decisions. As he took on a variety of projects that turned out not to be profitable, the debt nearly sank him. He had trouble keeping his commitments to charities and others.

Amid all the turmoil, he found that he was losing his business focus. His competitors had downsized quickly to deal with the new economic reality, but he did not respond quickly enough. He had several hundred employees, and he was paralyzed. He lost some of his key people, including a partner who had been bringing in a lot of business.

He and his family experienced unnecessary stress. Similar companies in his town fared much better, but he had put himself in a situation where he was operating from a position of weakness instead of strength. He had become entangled in projects and investments without sufficient knowledge of them. In short, he had no business being there.

The underlying problem was a lack of vision for what to do with the payoff—and that is a common scenario. Many business owners who are on the verge of a huge growing opportunity instead waste time dabbling in outside investments. The owner of a $50 million business might pull out $1 million and invest it elsewhere, becoming preoccupied with how that investment is doing day by day rather than keeping the focus where it belongs. As his mood rises and falls, the biggest loss is the opportunity cost. He drains his own business potential.

There comes a time in the life of a business and its owner when it feels like harvest time. The payoff seems to be coming after all the hard work. The challenge at such times is to keep the focus. This can be a dangerous time when the business can lose its way. People will show up on the doorstep offering all these supposedly great deals for how to invest that money: *"Don't miss this rare opportunity to make money in real estate!"*

That's no way to invest. Such decisions need to be based on established priorities, not on whatever comes your way. The vision needs to account for what to do when you finally get the payoff. Can you handle success? That essentially means making good decisions, which is the key to success in business and in life. In fact, you might say that what I strive to do now, in essence, is to help business people make great decisions.

—— GETTING TO THE NEXT LEVEL ——

The original vision by which a business owner gets started toward success is not always the same thinking that is necessary to get to the next level.

As you and your business grow, you need to revisit your goals. The vision can change. It is not necessarily all in place at the beginning. It needs to be sharpened, developed, and completed. Visions can run out of gas. A lack of making new commitments leads to the vision running out of gas. One client called it "out-kicking your coverage." Without refreshing your goals frequently, refocusing on the why before the what, you might find that you have exceeded everything you wanted to accomplish. That is truly a dangerous place, both professionally and personally.

Over time I have really come to understand how crucial that is. Years ago I started with a vision for my business and family, and I hit my objectives—but I did not yet have another set of goals in place, and so I was at risk of losing direction. I had written out a business plan, but I hadn't revisited it. You can lose your motivation and purpose that way. You end up just making and spending a lot of money, but to what end?

Throughout the life of your business, you have to have something that drives you. Generally, when business owners establish their first set of goals, they are in survival mode. They are in a situation where they know they must take certain actions if the business is to make it. These are decisions born of necessity, and that alone can be quite a motivator.

Once you attain success, that motivation can vanish. A lot of business owners try to stay scared. They might actually set themselves up to lose their money so that they can stay in that survival mode. They do not do it on purpose, and I'm no psychologist, but it does seem that people sometimes throw themselves into crisis to get back that feeling they had when the business was new. They like to be in a position where they are building from scratch. It is familiar to them, and they know how to do it.

I recently talked to a man who has a $70 million business—and he was facing a bit of a challenge. "I'm really good at digging myself out of holes," he told me, trying to reassure me, or himself, that he was putting a plan in place.

"I think you're really good at getting yourself into holes," I said. "So that's why you're really good at getting out of them." He knew I was joking with him, but he added: "You know, I think you just might be right!"

To get out of a situation requires a different kind of thinking than it took to get into it. What led you to success will not necessarily be what will take you to the next level. You need to rethink, refocus, and set those goals anew. If you must update your vision, then do not waste any time in doing so.

—— FINDING YOUR "WHY"——————————————

In my own career, I was beginning to lose focus in the late 1990s as dot-com fever swept the nation. I was feeling successful, both in my business life and in my family life. Each year, I would sit down and write our goals. I had them all set out for one year, three years, and five years.

I thought I was getting it all nailed down. In time, though, it seemed those goals became more financial, more of "let's get this, and let's have that." At one point I had several houses. I soon realized that it was time to take inventory of my life before all the "stuff" pulled me in a different direction I didn't necessarily want to go. "What now?" was the question and the answer I came to was that I needed to simplify.

This is something I see a lot in younger business owners. When we're goal-setting, they are perhaps more concerned with saying the right things. I often hear things like, "My top priority is my family/spending time with my wife/buying a home ..." but the fact is that they're working fourteen-hour days, talking about achievements and have also previously mentioned being rich, going on expensive trips, and material possessions like cars suggests otherwise. At one point in my younger years, one of my goals was literally to become a person who travels!

Your goals are your goals, and it's important to be really honest with yourself and identify exactly what it is that you want out of life. It's also important that you're clear and definitive about your goals. There is a saying that a goal without a timeframe is simply a dream, and this is true of course. If you do want to own a fleet of supercars, by when? If you're married or planning on marrying and/or having a family, at what point on your wealth building trajectory is that going to happen?

Behind all of this, though, needs to be an internal motivation. In my experience, when people focus on material possessions they don't find it very motivating in and of itself on a daily basis. Thinking of a car isn't necessarily going to give the energy, passion, and drive you need each day to steer your business in the direction you want it to go and overcome the challenges you might experience along with way.

So many of the good things that happen because of our goals wind up being by-products of the goal. And the by-products are a lot of times way better than the actual thing. For example, I committed back in 1999 to the Vice President at New York Life that I'd be the number one producer within seven years. That I'd win that trophy. And I hit it right on time. That in itself was cool, but it was all the things that built up to that that were more worthwhile. Learning what I learned, becoming who I became, the great travel experiences that I had because of that and around that, and the connections and people that I got to know and meet.

These aspects of achieving my goal are so much of a bigger deal to me now, looking back, than that accomplishment itself. That accomplishment was a check-the-box accomplishment, but it was all the things around it that were really interesting and continue to benefit me even now.

I still write down and revisit my goals on an ongoing basis, but they are different to what they used to be. They're far simpler. Now I establish what my commitments are, and what I want to make new commitments to. Once you start to do that, to create a vision that comes from within, your sense of purpose can develop and shift to a more positive and creative outlook, and as a result you begin making far better decisions. People typically find that being committed to certain things is far more fulfilling and can open their eyes to all the other possibilities that can come about as a result of making that commitment. Stuff serves as a distraction, whereas commitments refocus you on your *why*.

Life has taught me, progressively, the very lesson that I emphasize when working with business people: the *why* must come before the *what*. When you know why you are doing something, you attain a simplicity that helps you deal with complexities. If you are a business owner, you no doubt understand how complicated your financial affairs can become. You will be in a far better position to handle them effectively if you first identify your values and resolve to stand by them. It's only when you know *why* that you can see *what* you need to do.

—— WRITING OUT YOUR VISION ——

Over the years, three of my clients have made statements to this effect: "I want to do for my industry what Lexus did for the car industry." In fact, those were the exact words of one client. Another said he wanted to run his business the way Lexus is run—and when he bought his business, he also bought a Lexus to remind him of what he was trying to achieve.

In two of those three cases, the owners have accomplished what they set out to do, and the third is getting there. These businesses identified what it would take to meet their goals and build that value. They resolved to invest more in technicians and equipment without cutting corners. They emphasized the customer experience.

In short, they heeded the Lexus lesson, which is the pursuit of excellence at every level. As a result, like Lexus, their profits soared. They had identified precisely what it would take to drive those results, and they made their business investments and allocation decisions toward what would make the biggest difference.

It comes back to your vision. It takes dedication to a goal, which they defined as excellence at every level. It takes an engaged workforce that is on board with the goal. That's how you build a great business. Certainly it is important to conceive an exit plan by which the business someday will be sold or transferred to successors. First, however, you need to build something of value worth continuing. Keep that end in mind as you begin early to develop a business that will command a premium price and deliver the resources for a fruitful retirement.

Take a few minutes now to write down the vision for your business. You can use the form provided[1] as is, or use the form as a guide. Place it in your notebook or diary … somewhere that you can easily refer to it. Try to be as detailed as you possibly can, adding timeframes wherever possible. It doesn't have to be perfect, as we've said it will change with time, but at least

---

1. The form is also available on www.WealthonPurpose.com

starting to put your wishes for the future down onto paper will help you to think it through and outline it. Most of all it will bring clarity. There is a lot of power in clarity, and when you review your vision, as you often should, you can enhance that clarity. One day you will be able to ask yourself: Does this feel the way I wanted it to feel? Along the way, as you face a myriad of decisions, you will be able to ask yourself the same type of question: Do I feel good about this? Can I build on this?

WEALTH ON PURPOSE®

NEW BUSINESS OWNER ROADMAP™

DEFINE THE POTENTIAL.

What can be accomplished?

_____
_____
_____
_____
_____
_____
_____

Why do you want to do this and what's the most important aspect of it?

_____
_____
_____
_____
_____

Describe your vision on the ideal outcome.

_____
_____
_____
_____
_____

What has to be true when this is achieved? (Criteria)

1 _____
_____
_____
_____

2 _____
_____
_____
_____

3 _____
_____
_____
_____

4 _____
_____
_____
_____

5 _____
_____
_____
_____

BLUEPRINT TO ACTION

Action Initiatives to Meet and Exceed the
Success Criteria

ACTION INITIATIVE	BEST NEXT STEPS		
①			
②			
③			
④			
⑤			

When you have established a clear and written vision, then you can use it as a test upon which you can base your decisions. It will help you to say "no" more often to things that really will just be getting in the way. It will encourage you to say "yes" to whatever will advance the vision. With that vision as your beacon, you will be better able to assess the value drivers and line up the other details to which you must attend, deciding which are important and which are distractions. Such clarity can keep you from going down the wrong path.

The funny thing is, most business owners do live in the future tense. They think in terms of where they are going more than where they are. But only the most successful have a clear cut vision for their future. Many assume that having such a plan might stifle opportunities or they worry that if they take any pleasure in what they have done so far, they are afraid that enjoying it too much could knock them off track. Some people cling to the survivor mentality even when they are well beyond that stage. That feeling of hunger motivates them to grow—even though the stress can be bad for their health and keep their whole family on edge as well. That's why a clear vision can help so much: if you can see that you are on track toward your destination, then you will feel more confident in relaxing now and then, and enjoying the scenery.

Your vision, of course, involves more than the business. It involves your life. It involves your family. Along the way to achieving your objectives, you need to ask yourself: *What does this mean for my daily life? What does this mean for my relationships?* If you put a three-year deadline on an objective, for example, will that mean that you will not be home with your family for three years as you set about trying to accomplish it? How does that fit in with your overall vision? Are you truly on the path to satisfying the goal you wrote down?

Often, people will convince themselves of this falsehood: *I can't accomplish X unless I give up Y.* They believe that they must sacrifice one thing to get another. In truth, they are not accurately measuring just how much they are sacrificing. They are failing to see just how meaningless X might be when they have achieved it and don't know Y.

Instead, they might use their creative energy and adopt this attitude: *On the way to getting to X, can I make Y better? Can I make them work together toward my ultimate aim?* In truth, it takes no more effort to figure that out than it does to simply sacrifice the Y. To say yes to everybody but your family is hardly an easy choice. It's hard on your loved ones, and it is likely to be hard on you as well.

Having a clear vision for your future allows your brain to be more effective in helping you achieve what you want and your life will become simplified. When you decide on something you want, you are clear on when you want it, and you keep it front of mind, you will find that you naturally gravitate towards people, resources, and opportunities that can take you there.

The big question is this: *Where are you now, and do you like where you are going?* Is it time to make some big changes in your business and in your life? With an encompassing vision firmly in mind, you will be able to find your way through the forest rather than wandering among the trees. In fact, with a compelling vision, you can and will find a way to do what you want.

—— IN A NUTSHELL ——

The term Wealth On Purpose® is, of course, the title of this book, but it's also a trademarked process we lead our clients through. It has in it a double meaning that you will see throughout. It's about what to do once you have attained your wealth, but it is also about the *why* behind attaining it in the first place. It is about how you define success and pursue it intentionally.

If you don't know why you are doing something, can you really ever be sure you are successful at it? When you let the *why* guide everything you do, the *what* becomes clear. It is akin to beginning with the end in mind, as author Stephen Covey advocated, and it's also about finishing with it squarely in focus.

Once you have attained wealth, what will you do with it? At a certain level of affluence, most people want to match up their wealth with their values. When you no longer need to add to your lifestyle, how can you have an impact elsewhere? Unless you built your business just so you could pay the bills day by day, you likely are harboring some greater purpose.

Wealth On Purpose® is about identifying and developing that vision. Each of us has a heart for different causes. Some people want to correct wrongs, while others focus on advancing rights. Some have a heart for the poor, some for developing the arts, others for promoting education. Some have a deep-seated desire to save people. Whatever your inclinations and your values, be true to them.

Success comes from a deep belief in what you are doing and it also comes from happiness. I find that many wrongly believe that they will feel happy once they have achieved success, but without that success being clearly defined and without purpose and a vision to pull you towards it, happiness becomes evasive. I believe that successful business people can attribute their accomplishments to the depth of their purpose. I also believe that when they transfer that purpose to helping others, the world can benefit greatly from their passion. There is a wide universe of worthy causes. You can do the most good where you feel the greatest sense of purpose. Otherwise, your efforts could feel hollow.

How will you be remembered? What legacy will you leave so that what you have built will outlast you? This book continues to address those questions. Although these tend to be the considerations on people's minds at the end of a long and successful business career, I have placed this section first. As we strive for success, we need to keep a destination in mind. We need to identify our values and purpose so that we can bring meaning and passion to our life's work, thereby promoting even greater business success.

CHAPTER 2

MAKING A
— DIFFERENCE, —
TODAY

In a company's early stages, when it is in survival mode, the owner tends not to entertain the thought of giving their time or money away. It would seem to make little sense to further drain the resources that already feel stretched. It can be so easy to succumb to the pull of the future, where everything is brighter, easier, simpler, and more abundant, and forget that giving back is an important part of receiving, and is something that is a good practice for us all. Later, when the company is successful and making plenty of money, the owner may balk at the thought of giving away any more than the taxman already claims.

The issue with giving in the future or avoiding giving because you see it as a loss, of course, is that your day to day becomes about chasing ideals and about scarcity. While this mind-set can be hard to resist for those in an entrepreneurial frame of mind, it has to be balanced with some structure and planning, some self-ownership, so that our present life doesn't suffer. Most business owners I know got into business to achieve certain freedoms. They wanted to have more time to spend with loved ones and to do the things they love to do, they want to be able to choose their day-to-day tasks and do work they're passionate about, they want to provide for others and they want to feel fulfilled. Oh, and they want to be wealthy too. And if all that could happen yesterday, that would be great.

We all know this is an unrealistic expectation, that we can push ourselves too hard when we race ahead with impatience and ambition but little guidance. Giving back is important for cultivating the abundance mind-set which leads to wealth, because it keeps our focus on others, on our values, and on our contribution to the world around us. We must give in order to receive, and how we contribute our creativity and natural strengths are what our customers pay us for, so it's an important muscle to work out for all involved. It can also be tax efficient, which we'll explore in Chapter Five.

—— HOW WILL YOU BE REMEMBERED? ——

The other side of giving back is what you want to be remembered for. Your legacy. If you earn $1 million this year, you obviously do not get to keep it all. You get to keep $600,000 or $700,000, and the government lays its claim on the rest. That capital belongs to the government, which would become readily apparent if you tried to keep it. Another way to look at it is that this money will be put to use in our society, hopefully for the best.

We call that portion that you do not get to keep your social capital. The tax code is written in such a way that if you take personal responsibility for distribution of your social capital, you get a variety of great benefits. This is a key point that I try to make sure all my clients understand. The government has something to gain by giving you a tax break and letting you direct where your money goes. It does that to benefit society in general. And the tax code seeks to encourage certain desirable behaviors such as owning a home and investing for retirement and philanthropy.

If you do not take advantage of your opportunity to direct that social capital, the government surely will do it for you—but you might not agree with its choices. Instead, you can support the causes and institutions that are meaningful to you, imparting both your dollars and your values, and at the same time your family need not inherit a cent less.

—— CONTROLLING YOUR SOCIAL CAPITAL ——

If you have a $50 million estate, roughly half of what is left over after you have given a portion to your children will face an estate tax that, as of this publication is about 40 percent, but has in years past been much higher.[2] You get a lifetime exemption that, as of this publication, is nearly $11 mil-

2. Matthew D. Brehmer, "GOP Tax Reform Proposal," Crummey Estate Plan, June 2017, https://crummeyestateplan.com.

lion for a couple, but wealthy families still face a hefty tax obligation.[3]

Here's how that might break down: let's say that the $50 million is the amount remaining after you have gifted some assets to your children. About half of that will go to the government, and about half will go to your children. That's a lot of money going to taxes. You might call it a financial disaster. A nice way to say it is involuntary philanthropy.

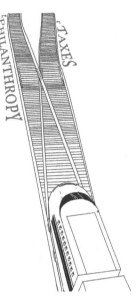

But that's not all. The government requires that it be paid in cash within nine months of your death. Many businesses have been forced to sell under less than optimal circumstances because of that requirement. The disaster worsens when a quick sale results in a far lower price than the family had anticipated that the business would be worth. The sellers need a quick deal, and the buyers know it. They're not going to be paying top dollar.

The Miami Dolphins once played football at Joe Robbie Stadium. It isn't Joe Robbie Stadium anymore. It was sold after his death. You can find many cases where it is very likely that property had to be sold because of the need for estate tax liquidity.

By contrast, you can plan so that you gain control of your social capital so that your philanthropy is voluntary. You might be able to arrange, for example, for your children to get the full $50 million, while at the same time creating $50 million for charity in a fund that the family controls. In that scenario, the family is controlling $100 million and advancing community interests—and all the while lowering current income taxes.

"That's a pretty complicated thing to arrange, isn't it?" people often ask after I explain this to them. And yes, dealing with wealth is a complex task, and it takes a vision to do this properly. The vision can be simple. For example, the Apple Air computer was the result of Steve Jobs' clear idea. He wanted a light computer that could fit in a mailing envelope but still do

---

3. www.forbes.com, article by Ashlea Ebeling, sourced: June 2017

everything that his current laptop did. Was it complicated to get there? Yes. In fact, the technology for what he wanted did not exist at the time. A year and a half later, it did.

That's the kind of vision that will produce results in matters of your estate, as well. "I want to do this. Let's get the people in place and do the things that we need to do to get there." Having that kind of clear vision is what cuts through the complexity to the simple core. That is how we got to the moon. The vision came first, and the details followed.

You have to know what you are driving for, and then everything can fall into place. My clients might not immediately see or understand these estate planning strategies, but once they see that they are possible and they have a clear vision, they generally will be pushing to accomplish as much as they can.

By taking control of the social capital, you leave your heirs in a great position to follow through on your values. You are teaching them about their role in handling wealth responsibly. They also learn about the value of sustaining wealth so that it can continue to be of real value to society.

This is your legacy. Your name will be synonymous with the contributions you made. It's more than the money, although the money does represent the time and resources and hard work involved in building anything worthwhile. But it is also the values that you have left behind, with your family and with your community. What perception will people have of you in a generation or two? Will you be recalled as one who contributed in meaningful ways? Or will they even remember your name?

—— WHY, WHAT, HOW ——

As we've discussed, the first step is to develop that vision, which you've hopefully now started to write out. Then you take a close look at your specific situation and see how much can be done. You may be surprised to find out that you can accomplish more than you thought you might. Once we then define the *what*, we can discuss the *how*. In other words, start by clarifying your purpose, then determine the desired result, and then work out the details to accomplish it.

Many well-intentioned plans get this syntax wrong. Unless your vision is based on a clearly defined and deeply meaningful purpose, the *what* is usually ill-executed at best. Sometimes life gets so busy, and you are so busy running your business, that you don't think about these kinds of things. You do not bring it up with your loved ones, and you do not bring it up in your own heart. As you focus on what you are doing, you don't pause to ask why.

To find out your *why*, you need to ask some big questions. Think of the things that matter most to you in the world, and in your world. Consider the meaning of money and the role you hope it will play in the life of your children. Do you have a personal philosophy or creed?

As you can see, there are very practical reasons not to delay developing your family wealth (and philanthropic, if any) goals. If you are at all inclined toward charitable giving, and most people are, then there is no time like the present. Consult with a professional who understands your situation and your business and can determine the most advantageous ways to apply charitable giving strategies, which take on a wide variety of forms—charitable remainder trusts, for example, and family foundations.

It is not my purpose here to go into all the details, which you can easily find fully explained in many sources, in print and online. Rather, I want you to imagine the possibilities and feel the excitement of how you can crystalize your objectives and best serve your business, your family, and your community.

In this way you will be creating a meaningful legacy for your children and grandchildren. We all have heard stories about how money can spoil the next generation. That's the problem with traditional estate planning, which doesn't think in terms of vision and influencing the community for the good. It's really a series of unpleasant business decisions meant to minimize cost, and then covering the cost typically with a life insurance policy. I'm not faulting anybody for doing that kind of planning because they generally do not know any better.

Family wealth preservation is very important, of course, but if the money transfers without a good set of values and virtues, it is likely to be lost anyway—in which case all the tax avoidance techniques that you put into place really didn't amount to a hill of beans.

I urge you to think more expansively, in terms of impacting the world with your wealth. When you do, you can gain options and freedom and a deeper sense of meaning and satisfaction. You really can do very well by doing good. Let's now go into the what and how in some more detail.

Part Two

BUILDING AND MANAGING
—YOUR WEALTH—

CHAPTER 3

NURTURING
—*Your*—
TEAM

Take away my people, but leave my factories, and soon grass will grow on the factory floors. Take away my factories, but leave my people, and soon we will have a new and better factory.

———

Andrew Carnegie

A baron of American industry, when asked to explain his great success, attributed it to his people. The above quote sums this up perfectly. The stories differ on just who that baron was, and it likely was an apocryphal account expressing a sentiment that any wise business leader would endorse: a company cannot survive without dedicated employees. As business leaders strive to build or maintain a highly successful enterprise, or as they prepare to sell it or pass it on to the next generation, they ought to be striving to do their utmost to enhance its value, based on the goals and the vision set forth. That is the goal of business wealth management—and it begins with nurturing those key employees.

A good management team makes a good business. These are the people who make the most important decisions, and their presence is essential in maintaining the value of the business. You need really good people. A company without good people will falter, and if something happens to the owner, who is going to step in to keep the company operating smoothly?

A valuable business is one that has been "de-risked." A potential buyer, looking to predict how an acquisition will grow, will pay more for a business if he or she perceives that it comes with less risk. If the business is driven solely by the owner, a would-be buyer will wonder what might happen once that owner is out of the picture. Will the clientele vanish? Are the systems only in his head?

Similarly, a business with only one or two key employees who have not been working there long will entail more inherent risk than one with several dedicated people of long standing who know the business intimately and have devoted a career to it. That is what I mean by a great management team, and that is what needs to be in place if a business is to be sold for optimum value.

—— MUCH TO GAIN, MUCH TO LOSE ——

Since a great team has so much to do with the value of your business, then clearly the converse is true: to lose key employees is to lose value. Without them, your business simply is worth less, and if that's not the case then those are not your key employees. Sometimes you can see the loss before it happens—someone will be retiring, for example—but it also could be a strike from the blue, as when a heart attack claims a life. Or you get a two-week notice of resignation, for whatever reason.

Generally, the latter scenario means that the key employee has been recruited away, to become somebody else's key employee. After all the work and training devoted to that person, he or she is gone in a flash. That leaves you in a position of vulnerability, and that is why this often is the first issue we discuss with new clients. Think about your own business. Are you vulnerable? What would be the result if something were to happen to you, or to a key employee?

Unless you operate a lifestyle business—which describes most small operations—it is generally a bad idea, hurts your business value and is far riskier if you depend upon just yourself or one other person. Many lifestyle businesses provide well for their owners and their families. I have clients who operate such businesses and are making $1 million a year or much more. Lifestyle businesses may have several employees, but they generally do not have key management teams. Generally, such a business is not sellable or valuable to anybody except the owner who operates it every day. The focus is not on retaining key employees, but rather on achieving goals to generate personal wealth that can be set aside for the future.

Those who operate a lifestyle business might decide at some point to grow it into something that could be of value to somebody else, whether a buyer or investors or heirs. You can make a decision to either stay a lifestyle business or to grow into an equity-focused business. This is really an investment decision. Should you reinvest cash in your business? Or is it better to take it all out and invest somewhere else? If you decide your business is a worthy choice, then it begins with people, and it is time to think in terms of key management.

As you become increasingly growth and equity oriented, you need to be thinking about those key people even if you do not as yet have a vision of transferring the business to somebody else. If your business is reliant solely upon you, you can only grow it to a certain point. You reach a ceiling. Dan Sullivan, my longtime coach, calls it a "ceiling of complexity" when you are at the level where you need to build a team around you, with each member doing what he or she is uniquely qualified and talented to do. These are people you certainly do not want to lose. It is at that point when further building will depend upon recruiting, rewarding, and retaining them. If the goal is to build a business that will command a good sales price, you can be sure that the new buyer will be taking a close look at that management team.

Your business will be even more valuable if that management team is motivated to stay on past the sale. A lot of owners make the mistake of rewarding their management team for building the value of the business and then do not reward them for staying through the sale. Everybody gets a big paycheck on the day of the sale. However, a key manager who gets a couple million dollars on the day of the sale may not stay put afterward. The buyer will likely be willing to pay a higher price for the confidence that the management team will be stable.

—— Financial incentives ——

How, then, specifically do you put in place the means to motivate the key managers? One way is to give them a stake in the desired outcome. That can be done in a variety of ways, including an equity stake or deferred bonus that is based upon getting certain things accomplished or reaching specified milestones. Such financial incentives can go far in motivating and engaging your managers.

Your key employees generally will be your higher-paid people—and the 401(k)s and pension plans and health benefits tend to be structured in a way that provides no special long-term incentive for key employees. In fact, the highly popular 401(k) by its nature discriminates against highly compensated people. Regulations limit the size of the benefits they can accrue in such qualified retirement plans. That hardly encourages the most valued employees to remain loyal to the company through the years.

As a solution, a business can set up non-qualified plans for those key employees. It can defer a portion of their pay in exchange for the promise of future benefits. The deferral of current compensation means that the key employees also will be deferring income taxes until they actually receive those future benefits. The plan also could include life insurance and other benefits. These can work particularly well in privately held companies. Other options include stock options, phantom stock, equity appreciation rights, and deferred or stay bonuses for keeping key people on through a sale or ownership transition.

—— A captivating culture ——

Beyond the financial incentives, another way to get your employees to stay is to develop a culture in which they are motivated because they get a sense of autonomy. They feel empowered to make decisions on their own, which cultivates in them a sense of purpose and meaning. That has been particularly important among the so-called millennials, those younger employees who emphasize quality-of-life issues more often than their elders did.

Much has been written about well-known companies with progressive and refreshing cultures. I have clients who are developing such cultures at companies in a variety of industries, including construction and software.

I know a business owner who has stated that his mission is to be the best in his industry. He is in the document management business, which at present means he deals in printers and copiers. He believes that the pursuit of excellence will lead to financial, career, and personal satisfaction for his staff. He gave his key employees a stake in the business and an ownership percentage, motivating them to look for the bottom line while focusing on customer service. His key people are enjoying incredible success, and they feel that they are doing something meaningful at the center of American enterprise. The culture builds on itself.

A successful company needs engaged employees. If the culture is troubled, you cannot put in place great plans or incentives. You cannot plan your way out of a dysfunctional company. If key employees do not feel engaged and motivated, then all the financial "incentives" that you give them will be seen as nothing but a ball and chain. Your offerings will be perceived as "golden handcuffs"—shiny, for sure, but ultimately shackling them against their will.

On the flip side, you can turn a functional company into a dysfunctional one by failing to plan and neglecting to establish the necessary incentives. It's similar to the way a functional family can become dysfunctional through failure to do effective wealth and estate planning, but no amount of it can make a dysfunctional family functional.

Steps toward engaging a workforce are spelled out in Daniel Pink's book, *Drive: The Surprising Truth About What Motivates Us*. He explains that employees need a sense of purpose so that they know why they are doing what they are doing, the right tools to get the job done well, and earn a sense of personal benefit and growth. Employees are happiest when they feel that they are growing right along with the company and that they have the freedom to influence the results. When writing out your vision, you might find that sharing it, or at least some of it, with your team has a positive impact on their behavior and attachment to the company. Part of finding the right fit in an employee is not just about their qualifications for the role and their ability to fit into the company culture, but also their values and whether or not they share yours.

── Managing with Trust ──

Micromanagers tend not to be the type to create giant companies, even when the vision is specific. Some say that Steve Jobs was a micromanager, but it seems to me that he was highly specific about the results, but not the path for getting there. He was clear and detailed and demanding about what he wanted to do and how soon he wanted it to be done, but he let his people figure it out. He did not care that the necessary technology did not yet exist. He knew that it was likely to come about if he set the goal with clarity.

Success requires implicit trust within the organization, and it needs to be horizontal among colleagues as well as vertical up and down the command chain. The owner or CEO needs to trust people, and they need to trust him. Otherwise, that sense of autonomy and purpose cannot develop.

You can run a company by fiat and force, like a dictator, and you can get results. The stick can be motivating. You can rule by fear. But that is not the style that will take you to the greatest glory, and those are not the results by which your company will blossom. That once was a prevalent style, particularly in factories where the foreman barked orders and people jumped. Today it is less common as companies seek to attract and retain creative employees. Companies depend upon that creativity to take them in new directions, and to effectively manage that mind-set requires a different touch.

There are many books and resources on organizational trust that share techniques and principles, but there are also many practical examples of CEOs of huge corporations (not just Steve Jobs!) using innovative ways of building trust across multiple, global, multi-level teams. Amazon CEO Jeff Bezos offers all of its warehouse workers $5,000 to quit, $2,000 if they're new, with a letter titled, "Please Do Not Take This Offer," Amazon rolled out their Pay To Quit program in 2014 and does this even when the company is in the process of adding new locations and making other changes. The thinking is that Amazon will be a more successful business with committed team members and losing the $5,000 to sort the wheat from the chaff is far better than the costs associated with retaining and investing in team members who are not committed to the growth of the company. It also shows a deep-seated confidence in the way Amazon manages, trains, and nurtures their warehouse employees—not very many must quit, as the scheme is still going strong.

Imagine if you turn up at your office tomorrow morning and your team has suddenly grown to several thousand people located all over the world. You wouldn't be able to use the same management techniques you currently use—you'd be forced to adopt new strategies. Try brainstorming some bigger picture ways of bringing people together and creating a unique company culture that nurtures and grows its best people. What could you do?

—— Don't forget yourself ——

A reward and retention plan for key employees that is professionally designed and implemented is a key to having a best-in-class management team. First you will need a culture that is conducive to such a plan, but once that is in place you will be able to make strides in improving the value of your company.

And as you make those improvements and build a solid management team, do not neglect to also treat yourself as the key person that you are and have a benefit plan in place for yourself. You need and deserve comprehensive strategies for tax efficiency and creating personal wealth for your family and heirs. In the next chapter, we will examine some of those strategies.

CHAPTER 4

CREATING
— PERSONAL —
WEALTH

Knowing how to manage the wealth that the business generates tends to be the focus of most of my new clients. They are actively running their business in a lot of cases and until they have that team support in place as we discussed in the last chapter, they may still be working in their business far more than they'd like to be. For many business owners, the daily running of systems, processes, and general management are not among the tasks they have the most mental energy for—most business owners would like to have a team in place handling all of that so that they are free to focus on strategy, publicity, partnerships, and nurturing top-client relationships. When a business owner is distracted like this and trapped amongst the weeds of their business, they can switch off to a degree and approach tasks on autopilot. As a result, their personal goals, purpose, and vision get stranded, separated from the physical management of the business.

However, it's important to bear in mind that your business, in its most basic form, is a wealth generator for you. Your business needs to be aligned with where you want to go in life and what sort of life you want to lead, with your business decision-making informed by your goals. Business wealth management, therefore, encompasses the opportunities through which you can see immediate progress towards your goals. No matter what stage of business you are in, this book is designed to help you focus on how the business can better the lives of you, your family, and your employees, and how it can be grown for a successful exit.

Typically though, when people come to see me, they are not talking philosophically about some of the matters this book highlights. Rather, they come with a specific problem they need help in resolving, or else they are on the cusp of the next opportunity and want to know the best way to seize it. Either way, they have a specific business issue at hand. Almost always, a great deal of business success results from eliminating the contingencies. By suppressing the bad things that might happen, you can make way for the good things. Therefore, sometimes the opportunity that business people are seeking to seize is how to eliminate the threat. It's the kind of preventative maintenance that keeps the machinery operating smoothly and efficiently.

Back in the 1990s, Bill Gates wrote a memo to his key managers that summed up the threats he believed his company was facing and what might be going wrong. The memo was leaked, and investors got the impression that he was panicking. Microsoft stock tumbled for a time. The reality was that Gates was hedging problems and trying to eliminate issues. The memo that listed all of the threats to the business was meant to communicate that he wanted them to be effectively addressed. That is part of why he has been so successful and consistently been ranked as one of the world's wealthiest people.

Gates was engaged in risk management. If this was paranoia, then at least he was using it productively. He was not acting in fear of the future, but rather in anticipation of it. Nonetheless, it took a while for the investors to regain their equilibrium.

I personally have long seen the value of being "productively paranoid." In the quest for success, a business owner needs to work toward eliminating whatever might get in the way of accomplishing goals. It's a matter of recognizing and controlling the dangers and risks. What I often have observed instead is that business owners actually add more risk to their companies and to their personal lives.

Even though most clients are keen to start talking about the specifics of wealth management, it all starts with vision, as the previous content highlights. You need to know why you do what you do, or it's all pointless. Nobody starts a business intending for it to be mediocre. Usually they start with the intention of taking themselves, their family, and their employees to another level.

Along the way, they define that level. Perhaps they are looking for more freedom and more choices. Perhaps they are hoping to find ways to truly impact their community. Sometimes the vision is as simple as not wanting their kids to have to go through what they went through themselves. In fact, I often hear business people express the latter. Once in a while, I meet people whose motivation is less idealistic. They carry a chip on their shoulder that drives them to success. They are out to prove something to somebody. It's a drive often born in childhood. They excel to dispel the label of mediocrity.

Whatever the source of the drive, the vision itself is positive. Even those who feel they have been done wrong are out to do something positive to counteract it. And so they, too, build an enterprise that contributes in some way to the world. They set out to achieve, and they eliminate the obstacles in their path. They knock down or find a way around the roadblocks to their success.

Through it all, successful business people strive to cut through the clutter and get back to the essence of why their business exists, the original goal they set out to accomplish. Keeping that firmly in mind, they are able to stay on track without spinning off into directions that dilute the passion. Ultimately, that is the wellspring of their success.

—— OPPORTUNITIES GONE WRONG ——————

A company involved in construction or in some aspect of technology will double down on an investment in its own industry that it perceives as a good opportunity. A biotech executive who is making a high income might decide to invest in a couple of cool biotech startups that he has heard about. They seem like sure winners. Soon those startups are needing a little more money than he thought they would require, but that seems okay because everything is going well in his own company.

But then the entire biotech industry turns south. Those startups that had seemed so promising are struggling and, without an infusion of cash, might go under. This is happening just at the time that the investor's own company needs to cut back because investors are pulling the plug.

It happens in every industry. The executives become enamored by the investment potential in some related field, and they invest in those related enterprises that they see making so much progress. Then the market cycle hits the entire industry, and those businesses shut down—and the investors feel a threat to their own survival.

Some advisors do suggest that it is a good strategy to put your eggs in one basket, but keep a very close watch on that basket. And there is wisdom in that approach. That one basket incorporates all the things you know how to do well. The issue is this: If it is your basket, then you can only "control the controllables." What you can't control is what other CEOs or the market or  the economy might do. Maybe the risk you are taking in your own business is enough. Think through what circumstances might take your business to zero. Then consider what might do that to those outside enterprises. Maybe your extra cash can go toward diversifying instead of compounding risk.

You may have significant expertise in a specific aspect of your industry, but know next to nothing about associated businesses. Knowing next to nothing is not a green light to proceed. When you branch out into areas that are not your forte, you risk falling flat. Not only do you risk losing a lot of money, but you also risk relationships. If you have invested in an associated business in your industry, it is likely that the owner of that business is one of your vendors, or perhaps you are a supplier to that business. Maybe you are fishing buddies. Perhaps even in-laws. Suffice to say that when things do not work out well, it's more than a monetary loss.

All business people need to focus on what matters most, and to invest their time and energy there. Getting sidetracked on an associated enterprise not only can over-concentrate your resources, but also can scatter your attention. Your job is attending to the big picture. Don't be distracted by lesser pursuits. I have seen owners of $100 million businesses who are spending much of their time fretting over a $5 million personal portfolio. If it does very well it might average 10 percent a year—but that is not even close to what they could bring in if they just devoted all that energy to their business pursuits.

Wealth creation is really a matter of allocating your energy appropriately. I'm not saying that the personal portfolio is unimportant, but rather to keep it in perspective. If you are confident about how you have positioned your business and are pleased with the status quo, then you can afford to divert your time and energy. Sometimes, however, business people respond to the discomfort of uncertainty by turning their attention to something that seems more controllable. The key is to build your team strategically so that you are not sucked in to fighting fires or responding reactively. Wealth building relies on your ability to react proactively.

—— WHAT IS YOUR END GAME?

Determining the proper approach to creating personal wealth has much to do with your business objective. In other words: What is your end game? Imagine you have "finished" your business—what does that look like? The answer to that question will tell you where to focus your efforts.

Let's say you have a lifestyle business that gives you meaning, purpose, and

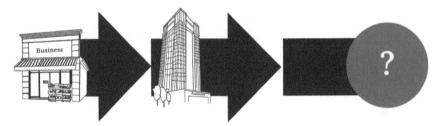

value in the community. You can make plenty of money that way, but the business will not be of value to anyone else. You won't be selling or transferring it. Therefore, your end game will be to retire on a portfolio of wealth that you build outside the business.

That means you will need to be tax efficient in your decisions, because taxes tend to be heavy for a lifestyle business. For example, a professional in California might be making $1 million a year but paying $450,000 in taxes. That makes it tough to save money while also enjoying a lifestyle that would seem commensurate with that type of income. Those taxes are likely to be the business owner's biggest bill each year.

As tough as it is to save money, however, it is essential that the lifestyle business owner does just that. Taxation needs to be managed for utmost efficiency so that money can be set aside for a prosperous future. Because your end game does not involve funding that future from the eventual sale of the business, your strategy becomes maximizing your current income, and then protecting and prudently growing the wealth that you are able to set aside.

You, of course, will be doing some of those same things if you are building a business that is more than a lifestyle, one that someone will be interested in buying. However, your emphasis also will be on minimizing or eliminating every single threat to your business that you can identify as you anticipate your endgame. Even if your business is larger than this, say you're pulling in $10 million plus in revenues and taking out $1 million a year, sometimes a little more to cover taxes, you might still be paying about as much in tax as you are spending, and the rest of the profit is going back into the business. Saving and managing your wealth for tax efficiency is still therefore a big priority.

INVESTING IN PEOPLE

Once you are clear on what you want your business to do for you, just as you need a key management team inside the business to handle affairs effectively, you also need a team *outside* of your business once you have started to create assets there.

To a large extent, this is about *staying* rich, rather than *becoming* rich. If your business success has brought you wealth, your advisor should be focused on helping you to preserve that wealth. This is not so much a matter of making you wealthy but of keeping you from becoming unwealthy. Look for financial advice that will help you to ensure that what you have gained will not be lost.

That can be a hard point to get across to people. I try to explain it with a graph, charting what happens when a business grows by a certain percentage and when a portfolio does likewise. The business growth is not taxed until you sell it, and it is generally a larger amount than the growth of the portfolio. That tends to illustrate where the business owners' focus should be. Meanwhile, they need to be confident that the outside investments are in the hands of the right people.

In the end, you are betting on people more than you are betting on systems or on other businesses. For example, I am in a private equity fund that invests in individual companies. I used to pick which ones to invest in, based on how much I liked the deal or the company. I had only average success with that approach. My personal involvement was not gaining me anything. Sometimes it was hurting me. I eventually learned to trust my co-investors, who were the best in the business. They knew what they were doing. They probably have a process that filters the best opportunities. My results became much better the more I trusted them without worrying about each deal.

That might feel counterintuitive, but it comes down to investing in people. That's what you are doing when you take steps to keep your key managers, the ones you trust to run your business well. And that's what you are doing when you place your trust in an advisor who you are confident will steer you the right way.

—— STAYING RICH ——————————————————

When my clients are making investment decisions, I review with them a variety of key considerations. One of the big issues is whether the investment will hurt them if it should take a dip in value at the same time that their business goes into a down cycle. In other words, could their outside investments be compounding a problem? Might it be better to purchase an investment that does not seem so correlated to the business, that doesn't generally rise and fall in tandem with it?

I also help them to think through whether the investment might end up as a liability. I used to buy a lot of investment real estate, and it always seemed to come with a set of liabilities. Whether or not you have a mortgage, you also need to consider the taxes and the upkeep. I found that the drain on my energy was a significant liability, and so I divested myself for that reason. The time and effort required to oversee it all was just not worth it to me.

You never know what you might face. A friend rented out his house in a nice neighborhood to a tenant who wanted it only for a week during an Austin music festival. In that time, the tenant built an ugly chain-link fence around the house. And before he left, he trashed the place, doing $45,000 in damage in one day. An extreme example, but certainly a liability to consider. You need to think about what comes along with an investment.

The liability can be more than financial. Personally I had three nice properties, and I felt emotionally attached to them. I found myself becoming overly upset about how they were treated, as in: "They broke a window that's been in that house for 100 years!" I couldn't take it. I got rid of those properties. When an investment becomes a drain on your energy, or a drain on your peace of mind, it's time to say goodbye.

You must think through your financial commitment. This is of particular importance with private investments. The potential return might be greater, but so is the potential liability if the business in which you are investing requires more capital. You may be asked to pony up during the worst possible time, when your core business needs money or when your liquidity has dried up due to an economic downturn or negative business event. The investment can get very hungry and quickly eat away your capital. When things go bad, they go bad fast. Private investments usually involve a lender, and banks get squeamish and try to pull out. Typically, they will have first dibs on the assets of the business.

To create personal wealth, you need to assess the potentials and the liabilities, both for your business and for yourself. Success requires the right positioning to take advantage of the cycles that come naturally in business and in life. You need to diversify in a way that will both advance and protect your interests, understanding that diversification does not guarantee protection against loss of principal.

If you own a high-powered, growing business, your investment needs are different than a typical employee who is saving money for retirement in a 401(k). The popular ways to invest that you might see on the cable news on a Saturday afternoon are geared toward a mass audience.

Remember: your goal is not just to get rich, but to stay rich. You need to avoid big mistakes and understand just how far your investment might fall, because it might be inclined to do so at exactly the wrong time. You might do well by cultivating a productive paranoia, a la Bill Gates. Make your investments with full awareness of everything that could go wrong, and eliminate as much risk as you can. Instead of jumping on the investment bandwagon, look for things that seem out of favor. They might be your best opportunities.

Generally, if you are going with the crowd, you are probably going in the wrong direction. To buy and sell based on emotion rather than analysis is likely to lead you to loss. A wise investor takes the time, with the help of a competent advisor, to think through what makes the most sense from both a business and personal perspective.

CHAPTER 5

TACKLING
— the —
TAXES

A business owner has what seems to be an exciting offer in hand for the sale of his life's work. He and his wealth manager sit down to go over the last minute details of the deal, and they start reviewing the math. As the numbers come into focus, the excitement fades. No matter how they crunch them, those numbers are just not going to add up to a successful retirement.

It is, sadly, a common scenario. Generally, it is because the tax bite is so much larger than the business owner had expected. Often the taxes will swallow a third of the value of the business. The standard of living that a $10 million transaction might have produced just does not seem possible when less than $7 million will be coming in.

And so the business owner backs out of the deal. "I can't do this," he says. "I need to get more money for the sale, or my family won't have even close to the support that we have now from the business." He decides that he will need to work a few more years and try to build the value of the business, and start over by finding another potential buyer.

It's not that the taxes come as a surprise. It's just that the tax figure always seems to come in larger than the business owner imagines. For example, the federal capital gains tax has been creeping up. Not that long ago, the highest rate was 15 percent. Now it's 23.8 percent (if you add in the new Affordable Care Act tax of 3.8 percent), and on top of that you have whatever percentage your state collects. Also, the gain or recapture on depreciated assets may be taxed as high as the ordinary income tax rate.

All of that needs to be carefully considered, as well as the fact that the final year before you sell your business will typically be your best. That's because you are trying to sell at the top, obviously, and not at the bottom—so even your income tax burden that year will be higher than normal. Clearly you need to take advance action to manage that situation.

Tax planning is an essential part of a broader category that we call windfall planning. By a "windfall," I am referring to a relatively rare event that produces a significant sum of money that will require special handling. Generally, that money represents the proceeds from the sale of the business, although we do have some clients whose incomes can spike so high that the same strategies come into play. The windfall could come from a highly profitable year, or the sale of property or of an equity interest. Sometimes, the windfall results from the sale of stock when an executive leaves a public company.

Managing a windfall requires specific strategies, and handling the taxes is a prime consideration. After all, those taxes can be a deal breaker, as we have seen, once the business owner runs the numbers and does the math. I have seen such scenarios play out.

Nonetheless, much can be done to mitigate that tax bite. We have had many clients who were able to negate all the taxes that come from selling a business. The same type of planning that can get rid of capital gains taxes also can diminish up to half of the income taxes.

—— The RIGHT MIND-SET

Taxes are a necessary part of life in our culture. They represent much of the social capital needed for society to function. However, you also are producing social capital when you donate to causes and institutions from your own resources. Therefore, it makes sense that the tax code allows you to do things that are good for society. To encourage your own contribution of social capital, the government provides the means for reduction of taxes, such as through charitable trusts, as we discussed in Part One.

You will gain a great advantage in that you get to deduct all of that contribution now against the sale of your business, or you can wrap it into a tax-free trust so that you only pay taxes when you pull money out.

That type of strategy requires careful planning. You do not want to just show up at your lawyer's office and say, "I want a charitable trust." First you need the mind-set and the vision—the *why*—after which you can figure out the *how* and the details for accomplishing it.

The proper mind-set is not as simple as: *I want to leave money to charity.* Rather, it is this: *I want to leave to charity the amount that otherwise would go to taxes.* The distinction is important. People can get off track at the prospect of leaving their business wealth to charity. They think of it as something they have built for themselves and for their children. They become more interested in what their social capital can do for charity when they think of it in turns of repurposing dollars that would go to the government, and, in doing so, increasing their personal net spendable income.

In other words, even if you do not see yourself as charitably inclined, it still might make sense to become charitably inclined when you can save on taxes, gain more control over your social capital, and increase your income. If you believe it is a good idea to reduce your tax bill, then why not also direct some of that savings to charity and also use some of it to enhance your estate for your heirs?

TOOLS FOR TAX EFFICIENCY: CHARITABLE Gifts

While it is beyond the scope of this book to detail the many paths of tax avoidance, let's take a look at charitable giving as an effective means of wealth management. My focus on charity is not just about the giving back and social capital we touched on earlier.

While we touched on charitable giving earlier in this book as an altruistic notion and to cultivate a growth mind-set, you can increase your financial wellbeing by giving to charity, too. Your net worth can actually go up through charitable planning. It can be hard to understand how that might be so, and often when I explain this to people they first seem rather incredulous. How could it be, they wonder, that in two situations in which all else is equal, the person who does more advance planning with gifting will end up with a higher net worth?

With some creative thinking and some insightful use of the tax code, the resources that might have gone to the government through tax can be put to immediate use for charity. The simplest way is to donate a small portion of the asset that is creating the wealth. That creates a tax deduction, reduces the tax bite every year, and increases cash flow.

As mind-boggling as it might seem to some, that is how the tax code has been written from the beginning. The provisions were modified a great deal in 1969, and what we have now is what has been in place since then, with only a few changes. As taxes have risen a bit recently, this type of planning has become even more meaningful than it used to be.

Let's examine a couple of scenarios of how giving to charity helped two different types of people achieve their stated vision. In the first instance, a wealthy couple with assets of $100 million or $150 million wanted to leave some amount to their children but not enough to make them super rich. Instead the couple wanted to contribute toward making this world a better place, but they did not want to wait until they are dead to donate that money. They wanted to find an efficient means of charitable giving so that they can see, while they are alive, the difference that they are making.

At the same time, they do want to help the family—and the family is more than their children. There's the family at home, and the one at work. They want to do right by the employees of the company they built, as well as their own flesh and blood. Giving to charity, however, does not mean short-changing either of those families. "Charity begins at home," the adage says, but it certainly need not stop there, and it need not wait until you have passed away. Philanthropy is a practical wealth management strategy: it is a tool that can benefit your portfolio at the same time that it benefits society.

In the second instance, a client once owned a construction-related business that was accumulating cash and they were living well within their means. In fact, their accountant had told them that the excess cash in their business could result in a tax penalty. That was one issue they were facing when they came to me for guidance. They also intended to pass the business to their children and wanted to do so as efficiently as possible.

Working with their accountant and attorneys, we decided on a strategy that gave a significant part of the businesses to a charitable remainder trust, from which the couples would get an income for life. Then they were able to use the accumulated cash to purchase that part of the business out of the trust. As a result, the charitable trust now had cash, which was enough to provide them a steady income for the rest of their lives.

Meanwhile, they transferred to their children the portion of the business that had been in the trust, along with the portion that they had kept out of it. So now the children owned all the business, and their parents had an adequate retirement income for life.

The strategy spared the couples from paying the excess cumulative earnings tax, which would have been 50 percent of the millions of dollars they had on the books. Instead, they got a tax deduction for several million dollars—and they paid no capital gains.

This is an example of how careful wealth management can save millions of dollars and preserve a family business that otherwise might have been lost to outside interests. Again, it begins with a clear, compelling, and simple vision statement. It must be concise enough so that the end result is easy to see.

For those couples, the vision amounted to this: "We want to build up our company and save enough so that we can give it to our kids and retire comfortably while they run it." To which I asked them a few questions:

"How much have you saved up so far for retirement?"

"Not much."

"Well, are you charitable by nature?"

"We would like to be, but we do not want to hurt ourselves or the children by giving our money away." And I commonly hear that. People want to do more, but they are concerned about the charity that begins at home. They see their wealth as a pie and worry about slicing it up. They do not realize that philanthropy can produce benefits for all.

Once these clients grasped the possibilities, they were able to restate their goal: "we would like to be secure in retirement and see the business go to the kids, and instead of paying taxes, we would like as much as possible to contribute to the charity of our choice." They had recast the vision, but essentially the goals were the same. We were just able to do it in a much more exciting, more fulfilling, and more financially efficient manner.

In another example, we worked with a relatively small business that has a couple of million dollars of cash flow and is worth $12 million. We set up a scenario where we give $1 million worth of the business, or roughly 8 percent, to charity. That $1 million deduction produces a savings for the year of $400,000 in taxes. Also, moving forward, the business will be taxed annually not at $2 million, but at 8 percent less than that. And at the time of sale, there will still be a tax savings on $1 million of capital gains.

If this was you, you have now earmarked $1 million for charity, and if you want you can buy that back in the future. With planning done properly, that buyback can be in a trust for your children and grandchildren. That's now producing a gift or estate tax savings of up to 40 percent. That's in addition to all the income and capital gains tax savings. You are now creating a cash flow that you can use for charity, or for other purposes depending upon what you decide will make the most difference. Some donors will ease into their charitable giving strategy, while others have a goal and want to fund it immediately.

That strategy of donating hard assets such as business interests and real estate is simple and effective, although it is rarely used. Statistics show that about 80 percent of gifts are from cash and only about 20 percent are from assets. However, much of the charitable giving potential lies in the opposite scenario: 90 percent of wealth consists of assets, and only 10 percent is cash.[4] If people understood that those assets, too, could be a source for philanthropy, they could make a far greater impact.

A common question from business owners is this: "If I give to charity now, doesn't that mean my family will get less someday when I sell my business or transition it?" It is important to consider that if you donate $1 million from your business to charity, that in effect creates $400,000 of new wealth for you, and when you pass away it will not be taxed. If instead you leave that million dollars in your estate, it will be heavily taxed. For instance, the top estate tax rates have ranged from 45-70 percent.[5] With charitable planning, your family can save a significant amount in estate taxes. Your gift also will mean that when you sell the business, you won't have to pay the capital gains tax on that million dollars.

Let's look at all three taxes that would have been levied on that million dollars before you gave to charity:

—— SCENARIO 1: ——
LEAVE $1 MILLION IN YOUR ESTATE

Under the first scenario, you keep the million dollars of business value in your family. When you sell the business, you will pay a capital gains tax on that million dollars of 24 or 25 percent. That leaves you with $750,000. If you have that money when you die, it will be subject to an additional 40 percent estate tax. You then have $380,000 remaining.

4. "Give More By Giving Wisely," National Christian Foundation Houston, 2015.
5. Julie Garber, The Balance, June 2017, www.thebalance.com.

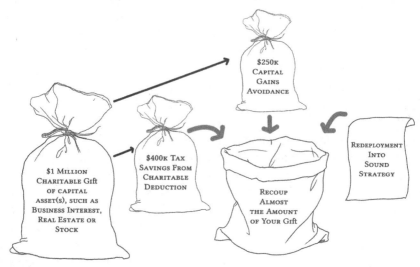

— SCENARIO 2: —
DONATE $1 MILLION OF THE BUSINESS TO CHARITY

$250K CAPITAL GAINS AVOIDANCE

$1 MILLION CHARITABLE GIFT OF CAPITAL ASSET(S), SUCH AS BUSINESS INTEREST, REAL ESTATE OR STOCK

$400K TAX SAVINGS FROM CHARITABLE DEDUCTION

RECOUP ALMOST THE AMOUNT OF YOUR GIFT

REDEPLOYMENT INTO SOUND STRATEGY

DONE UNDER EXPERT GUIDANCE

Under the second scenario, you donate $1 million of the business to charity. You immediately realize a tax savings of $400,000 from the charitable deduction. In addition, you won't be paying any capital gains tax when you sell, so you will be realizing a tax savings there of about $250,000. And you will not be paying any estate tax on that money. In other words, if you think about what you could earn on the tax savings by redeploying it into a sound strategy, you have almost recouped the amount of your gift.

We have, at times, helped business owners repurpose the cash flow that they gain and use it to purchase life insurance, if that helps them to achieve their goals. For example, the business might need protection in case it would be hurt in the event that the owner died. The owner's family also might need income protection. In addition, the life insurance payout also could be used in the estate planning. For example, it could be used to equalize the estate if the owner has several children but only one of them will continue to be involved in the business.

It's not just about leaving money to charity. It's about leaving money efficiently to charity. You could just write your will to bequeath your assets to charity—a highly inefficient approach but one that's done all the time because people tend to be more charitable minded than tax smart. If they were tax smart about their giving, they could have twice as much to give away if that was what they wanted to do.

The methods are many and varied. There are about twenty-five paths you could take. The key is in putting together a team that can implement your vision, design it, carry it out, and maintain it.

This planning needs to begin well before the sale of your business is imminent. It's a holistic plan. You do not just become a philanthropist in a vacuum. You do it in light of all the other factors in your financial life and personal life. The tax issues need to be fully considered, of course, but you also need to identify the charity or charities that you will want to assist. And it needs to dovetail with your personal financial plan, which we will be discussing in more detail shortly.

One of the tools that we commonly use in a relatively simple plan is a dual trust mechanism. One of them is a charitable trust that saves all the capital gains taxes, provides an income tax deduction, and generates an income for life. Eventually all of the assets in that trust will be going to charity, so we also set up a wealth replacement trust. This one will go tax-free to your children or other heirs. There's no estate tax or capital gains tax, and you have control over the amount of income tax you pay. When you compare that dual trust strategy to the status quo, the tax saving is about 60 or 70 percent. It produces a higher income, and it can preserve wealth for generations.

Philanthropy is a noble pursuit, but there also are very practical reasons to pursue these strategies for your personal wealth gain and for the efficient transition of your business. You can also discuss DST and ESOP, business owned real estate, deal structure, earn out or installment sale rules with your trusted advisor.

—— TAX AVOIDANCE, NOT EVASION ——

Strategies such as the above certainly result in tax avoidance, but by no means do they amount to tax evasion. This is how former Supreme Court Justice Louis Brandeis explained the distinction in his essay, "Thoughts on Legitimate Tax Avoidance":

> *I live in Alexandria, Virginia. Near the Supreme Court chambers is a toll bridge across the Potomac. When in a rush, I pay the dollar toll and get home early. However, I usually drive outside the downtown section of the*

city and cross the Potomac on a free bridge. This bridge was placed out-side the downtown Washington, D.C. area to serve a useful social service: getting drivers to drive the extra mile to help alleviate congestion during rush hour.

If I went over the toll bridge and through the barrier without paying the toll, I would be committing tax evasion. If, however, I drive the extra mile outside the city of Washington and take the free bridge, I am using a legit-imate, logical and suitable method of tax avoidance, and I am performing a useful social service by doing so.

For my tax evasion, I should be punished. For my tax avoidance, I should be commended. The tragedy of life is that so few people know that the free bridge even exists!

In other words, tax avoidance is legal, tax evasion is not.

When you strive diligently to avoid taxes by legitimate means, you perform a useful societal function that the government recognizes. The government put those bridges in place in hopes that enough people would drive the ex-tra mile to ease the congestion of tax funded services. You can be sure that the government also will be keeping an eye on whether you are doing this right. That is why it is advisable to have expert guidance on tax matters.

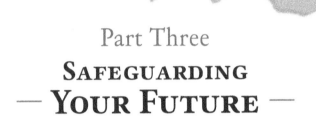

Part Three

SAFEGUARDING
— YOUR FUTURE —

CHAPTER 6

WINDFALL
— PLANNING —

By windfall, I mean the significant sum of money that you hope will be coming into your hands when you sell the business. Windfall planning also could involve the sale of real estate, or an inflow of money from some other source, but in our context we generally mean the sale of the business.

Windfall planning involves reducing the uncertainties, such as how to deal with taxes. You will only be selling your business once. It's a big event. Half that money can go away due to taxes, so that must be a major emphasis of the planning. The other emphasis is how to make what remains sufficient to support you for the rest of your life. You need to plan for a lifelong income with sufficient growth to see you through what could be decades of retirement.

You also may wish to have a significant amount left over as a legacy for future generations. In that way, business wealth management and windfall planning both tie back to Wealth on Purpose®. Legacy issues are a major part of windfall planning. So how should you be thinking about selling your business and what are the tips and traps to be aware of?

—— HOW DO YOU GET OUT? ——

I have talked to many business owners in their late fifties or early sixties who are wanting to develop a strategy for how they will exit the business that has long provided them with a nice lifestyle. They have found success, by any measure, and yet they often feel confused about what an exit looks like. Even though the business has brought them a good income, they are concerned that it would not sell for an adequate amount so that they could invest the proceeds and sustain their lifestyle in retirement. In fact, that's very common.

In other cases, business owners are concerned about how to deal fairly with partners in the business. They are wondering how to coordinate the exit so that all the partners are on the same page and ready to make the commitment. I have worked with businesses on various occasions in which two partners have differing ideas about that. One might want to sell while the other wants to pass the business on to the children. How do you resolve the conflict in a way that works for everyone?

Tax considerations are a big part of the reason they may be concerned that they might not receive enough money to sustain their retirement. In large part, however, the problem is that they have not done the necessary things to make the business valuable enough to an outside buyer.

I can work with business owners on both of those concerns by customizing their plans with a set of tools specifically designed to build business value. The details of such planning can seem complicated without a highly specialized advisor in these areas. Succession planning (sometimes called transition or exit planning) must be orchestrated so that the seller, the buyer, and the business itself can move forward efficiently. If succession planning is done well, the business owner will be able to realize the value that he or she has spent years building.

This process amounts to reducing risk. A business is more valuable if it is less risky than a comparable business. When you de-risk your business, you are less likely to lose money and therefore can move forward with the kind of confidence that promotes growth. The business becomes less stressful and more enjoyable to operate. The cash flow improves, which has much to do with enhancing the value for a potential buyer. Ultimately by improving the price-to-earnings multiple, you will get the best deal.

In working with clients, we develop a business wealth profile that helps them focus on a perspective and strategy for success. The exit planning needs to be done in conjunction with an overall personal wealth strategy. A major part of that is to understand the key value drivers of your business, as I will explain later in this chapter. That will get you to the point where you can draft a targeted succession plan for how and when you are going to exit your business.

Not all exits are planned, however. Sometimes the owner passes away or becomes incapacitated and unable to continue operating the company. Therefore, while designing a targeted succession plan, you need to also have a plan in place in the event of such a contingency. That contingency plan should dovetail with the targeted plan. With proper preparation, both your exit plan and your contingency plan will be similar in nature. After all, a contingency is a risk, and your exit plan involves de-risking your business. By doing the latter, you are effectively dealing with those contingencies that might arise.

—— THREE PATHS OF SUCCESSION ——————————

Essentially, your successor will be in one of three categories: an outside buyer, an inside buyer, or a transfer or sale within the family. Each of those options requires a different strategy.

- Succession within the family generally means that the owner is leaving the business to one or more of the children, either giving or selling it to them.

- Sale to an insider often means that a key employee or group of managers will be taking the reins, or perhaps it will be sold to an employee stock ownership program (ESOP).

- An outside buyer would be another business, perhaps in the same industry or perhaps a private equity fund.

Well before the time of sale or transfer, the business owner needs to focus on what would make the business valuable to an outsider. By enhancing that value in the eyes of an outside buyer, you are also doing so in the other two succession paths—that is, to an inside buyer or within the family.

Whatever would raise the potential sales price to a strategic or investment buyer will also make your business more valuable to a key employee or to your children. This is a valuable exercise for all businesses, regardless of the exit plan, because what makes it valuable to an outsider is also what makes it valuable to the owner.

It is essential that you not get too close to your exit date before working on these matters. You need time to adequately address any issues that could be diminishing the value of your business. If you're selling within the family, you also need to start planning early to train the successors who will be managing the operations. They have to learn the business inside and out, and that takes time. The business owner may even have a "no-exit exit" in which he builds the business in such a way that eventually he no longer is needed on site and becomes just an investor in it. He no longer shows up to work there, and he no longer runs the business, but it is an income-producing asset for him. He has taken the steps to make the business more valuable and to train a successor management team that can continue on without him.

I have found that key employees or employee groups generally do not have the ability to write a check to you for the business. They would love to own part of the business, but they do not have the capital to purchase it. So the business has to be set up in such a way that it can "cash flow you out," either because the business can borrow the money to buy you out now, because it's so strong, or because you're going to finance it with a nice arrangement for yourself, or the key employees or an ESOP purchase it from you.

ESOPs can be effective because significant tax benefits could be available both to the business and to you, the seller. Sometimes those tax benefits create a cash flow that makes this the best successor option. Those same tax benefits, by the way, can make ESOP-owned companies much more competitive than other players in this market. They are able to earn more profit, and therefore, invest more of their earnings back in the business.

One of the goals, of course, is to keep the company strong and competitive even after it is outside of your ownership. You want the best possible sales price, but you do not want to hurt the business in the process or hamstring your children if they are taking over. It starts with ensuring that the business is strong and competitive to begin with. Your business needs to be generating enough cash.

For example, let's say a private equity buyer writes a check for $20 million for a business. That buyer also will be writing a second check, which will be for operations. This is what you would think of as working capital. When you sell a business, generally you take all the cash out of it and sell the business itself. You do not sell the cash along with it. In other words, if you have $5 million of cash on the books, that doesn't go along with the sale.

It comes down to this: the smaller that second check can be, the more the value you are likely to get in that first check. A healthy business will be generating cash and require less investment going forward; and, therefore it is worth more.

—— VALUE DRIVERS ——————————————

You have a dual need. You want your business to generate enough money so that it sells for a price high enough that you can live well for the rest of your life, and you also generally will want the new business owner to see the potential for a profitable enterprise. The deal needs to be beneficial for both the seller and the buyer.

The conventional thinking is that if you get the highest price you can, you will be leaving the business in a worse situation—but that is not true. Instead, whether the business will thrive depends upon what we call "value drivers." A buyer generally will have three or four of them primarily in mind.

I have invested over the years in a lot of private equity businesses as part of the buyers group, and in doing so, I have often received memos explaining the main value drivers for a particular company from the buyer's perspective. Every business has several drivers that all businesses share, although certain ones are more important than others. Those are the ones that create the most cash and make the business most profitable and therefore worth the most to a buyer.

Work on an exit plan as early as possible, and working on these value drivers is of prime importance. Begin doing this as soon as your business has the ability to make investments in itself. It needs to work toward making more money consistently with less risk. It will require less capital, and it will be easier to borrow money.

A fundamental value driver is financial performance. The buyer of the business will be looking at the books and trying to see clearly how the business has been performing. If the books are not easy to understand, or if they are messy and mixed with personal expenses, the perceived value will be lower. If the balance sheet doesn't seem strong, the prospective buyer will be discounting the value of the business. We suggest to a lot of businesses that they get their books audited as a means to instill more confidence among potential buyers.

Curb appeal is another driver. If a buyer is going to pay $50 million for something, it had better look like it's worth $50 million. In other words, besides cleaning up the books, you need to start cleaning up the windows. You will need to have audited books for at least two years prior to the projected date of your sale. That means you need to be thinking about these matters at least three years before you expect the sale to take place.

Another value driver at which buyers will be looking is the company's growth strategy. This is highly important, because even though investors will be getting results that you have attained so far, that is not what they are purchasing. They are purchasing the potential for new results. They are buying the business with the expectation that it will grow further. That means that to show value to a buyer, you have to have a growth strategy, and you need to be experiencing some growth. The more of each that you can establish, the higher the multiple that you will get.

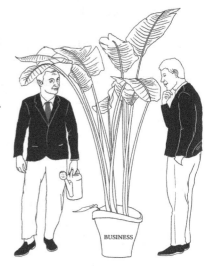

Recurring revenue is another driver. This makes a business more valuable because it is a cash flow that can be expected to continue regularly. For example, a software business can gain recurring revenue by obtaining service or support contracts. There are many models for recurring revenue. For example, if you buy a coffee maker that requires its own brand of refills, you are investing in that manufacturer not only when you buy the coffee maker but also every time you buy refills. You have purchased more than coffee. You have purchased a dedication to a particular brand.

Contracts are a great form of recurring revenue. If you do business with cities and they have a contract with you that they renew every 10 years, you have a pretty good deal. Cities are fairly reliable at paying their bills. Subscriptions are another recurring revenue model. Magazines are an easy example. Lately I even have been getting my razors as a monthly delivery. And people are becoming increasingly familiar with online subscription arrangements.

Another key driver is size. The bigger the business, the more it is worth. The value is rising not in proportion to the size but rather because the multiple gets higher as the business gets bigger. A bigger business, by its nature, is less risky than a smaller one. A smaller business is dependent on fewer people, perhaps even on one person. A larger business is dependent more upon systems and processes, and the risk is spread out among many people. The buyer will perceive this as a de-risked business and for that reason likely will be willing to pay more.

In financing the sale of a larger business, a bank generally will be involved—unlike deals for small businesses, which tend to be financed by the seller. The bank, of course, will be examining the level of risk involved in the transaction to determine how much it will be willing to lend as a multiple of cash flow.

Those are some of the major drivers for most businesses: financial performance, curb appeal, growth and growth strategy, recurring revenue, and size. A potential purchaser or successor will be looking at all of those drivers that add value to a business. These are the tools by which a business can build to a higher level to generate personal wealth and security. These are the means by which you pursue the vision, transforming it into a reality.

—— CONFIDENCE AMID UNCERTAINTY ——

The question is not simply, a*re you happy with your business?* Rather, think of it in terms of the "Dan Sullivan question," which is: "If we were having this conversation three years from today, what would have to have happened over the last three years, both personally and professionally, for you to feel happy about your progress?" The question helps to develop vision and clarity about exit options.

Having coached me for many years, Dan Sullivan helped me to gain crucial perspectives as my business grew ten times in size. I often ask my clients the "Dan Sullivan question" because I want to find out whether they are working toward a clear future. Sometimes they don't have an answer. That tells me that they don't have a vision and haven't even begun to think in those terms. Frankly, that's dangerous, and it means I might not be able to help them.

Succession planning comes down to this: Are you doing the most with what you have, so that you can get the most out of what you have done? That is a pertinent question for business planning, and it is a fundamental question for life. With a solid plan, it's much more likely that you will arrive at the destination you desire.

In his book *Great by Choice*, Jim Collins tells the tale of the 1911 race between Norwegian explorer Roald Amundsen and Robert Falcon Scott, a Briton, to reach the South Pole. Their expeditions are a study in leadership styles. As they headed into harsh uncertainties, they both had their plans and their great intentions, but Amundsen de-risked his journey. He anticipated what could go wrong, and he had a plan in place for those contingencies. Scott's plan amounted to: *if everything goes right, we will make it.* Amundsen was the one who made it. Scott and everyone in his expedition perished.

Whatever endeavor you are exploring, the lesson could not be more clear: if you want to make it, you need to de-risk your journey. That's how you attain confidence amid uncertainty. When you keep the end in mind and examine all your choices along the way, you are far more likely to succeed.

Chapter 7

Set
— For —
Life

The ultimate question for most business owners is how can they make sure that the company, which has been spinning off a good income for years, will continue to serve them that way once it has been transformed into a pile of cash. By whatever means, that money needs to be managed carefully so that you are set for life.

The sale of your business is a windfall that could represent your life's work, and it also represents a new direction for you in retirement. You have long depended on the proceeds of the company for reliable income to raise a family and build for a future. Now the sale is over, and that future can feel undefined. You wonder whether you will have enough money, after the toll of taxes, to produce a lifelong income that maintains your accustomed lifestyle.

The long-range view

The planning needs to begin long before receiving the windfall—if you wait until afterward, you can hardly call it planning—and your perspective needs to range far into the future. While you are operating your business you need to have a clear understanding of its value, of course, but also clear steps for translating that value into a lifetime income. What do you plan to do with the rest of your life? You need to figure that out before you take the step of retiring.

Do not underestimate how long that retirement might be. You could be depending on the proceeds from the sale of your business for considerably longer than you actually operated that business. I have met business owners who wound up with not nearly enough income. One owner, after the sale of his business, had a guaranteed income for life of $125,000. That was in 1981, and he could not imagine that he would ever need more than that. Well, he is still alive—and he could tell you that $125,000 is not what it used to be.

He sold that business when he was in his fifties. Today he is in his eighties, and he has had to start two more businesses—not what you would call retirement, and certainly not what he had planned to do. And that's another key consideration in ensuring that you will be set for life. Inflation will surely take its toll. You need to plan for the potential that you will live many more years.

That means getting the best possible deal on the sale of your business and then investing to preserve your nest egg for a lifetime. Certainly you will want a deal that is structured so that the company that you nurtured so long will continue to thrive, and generally you will want your successors to have the wherewithal to continue on your path of success. Nonetheless, the deal needs to be in the best interest of your own financial future—and that could be a long one.

Income streams for retirement can come from many sources, of course, and all must be considered when calculating whether you will have sufficient resources to meet your objectives. Besides the lump sum from the sale of the company, some business owners also negotiate income sources such as deferred compensation agreements or consulting contracts.

Those options will be part of how you structure the sale or transfer. For instance, an outside buyer may pay more for your business if you accept a contract to pay you a salary for the next ten years. That structure, in a sense, gives the buyer a form of financing. The buyer will not have to pay that portion up front.

There are many ways to get "paid" that also can help your successors, particularly if they are your children, run the business successfully, while also ensuring that your retirement proceeds successfully as well. The key is to keep an eye on the long-range view and not lose sight of the purpose you have set forth for a retirement filled with accomplishments.

A TRANSITION OF ATTITUDE

A buyer, from an outside perspective, generally will be seeing more risks in the business than the owner perceives from an inside perspective. Business owners tend to see less risk in running their own company than they would see if they were investing an equivalent amount of money in the market. That is because their business gives them a sense of control. They are familiar with it and understand its workings.

When you retire, you are transitioning from something that you control to something that you do not control. This is a significant adjustment not only financially but also mentally. Business owners who have been accustomed to pulling all the strings may feel that they have lost that sense of oversight, and it can be quite disconcerting.

Think again of the vision. Windfall planning involves three primary questions: *What will you be doing for yourself? What will you be doing for your heirs? What will you be doing with your social capital?* In Chapter Five, we examined how attitudes change once people define charitable giving as a means to save on taxes instead of a slice of the pie that they won't be leaving to their children. The taxation is a central consideration. They see that through careful planning, they can gain a great deal of control. Before my clients are educated on their options and how to plan effectively, they tend to associate retirement with a loss of control. In many ways however, you can have more control than ever.

TESTING THE SCENARIOS

Preparation is essential to successfully planning for a long and prosperous retirement. An effective means of preparing is to pose a variety of scenarios and to test the conditions that could advance or diminish your prospects for success.

This is done by thoroughly examining your retirement wealth plan, looking for anything that could get in the way of your objectives. That is a matter of putting the plan to the test. How would it fare, for example, during an economic meltdown such as occurred in 2008 and 2009? What would the effect upon your wealth have been if you had sold your business in 2006 and then went through that market turbulence?

We can get very specific on the potential outcomes as we stress test your financial plan. We can use software that charts the results of various scenarios, but a calculator works well, also. It's not hard to figure out what a 30 percent loss looks like.

Once we see the potential risks that a scenario presents, we can take action to protect the portfolio. We can look for financial products and services that will hedge those issues for you. We can point out approaches that will make the most out of whatever conditions are at hand so that you would be doing relatively well no matter what happened in the economy and in the markets. We can develop a variety of financial structures, which could include guaranteeing some of your income.

Again, remember just how long you might live after you decide to sell your business and retire. You or your spouse easily could live thirty years or more, and your income stream needs to last that long as well—and grow sufficiently so that your portfolio is not overcome by inflation. Your need for a sufficient gain to maintain your purchasing power means that your portfolio will require a reasonable level of risk. You cannot play it completely safe, but you need to keep that risk firmly under control.

Successful business people tend to be very good at eliminating risk, and they need to continue that mind-set even after they have sold the company and are investing in the market. Managing a retirement portfolio is not about getting the best return or beating some index. Solid and reliable growth is much more important. In the long run, you will be ahead if you do not lose money, even if that means sacrificing some of the growth when the market is rising. The emphasis needs to be on protecting capital and protecting income. Yes, you need sufficient growth to keep ahead of inflation—but you can get growth without taking as much risk as most people think is necessary.

Think of it this way: In the last thirty years, what were the best investments you could have made in the public markets? I ask people that, and no one knows the answer—and how are they going to know the answer going forward if they do not know the answer going backward? Hindsight is 20/20. If you go to the stockbrokers, they're going to say, "Stocks. Stocks. Buy stocks."

A better bet during that timeframe would have been bonds. The safer the bond you bought in the last thirty years, the better you did. If you loaded up on thirty-year treasuries three decades ago, you were paid around 11 percent a year. If you bought municipal bonds, you did even better. The relative performance of stocks and bonds is an example of how public perceptions are not always in alignment with reality.

—— AHEAD WITH CONFIDENCE ——

When weighing the proper amount of growth for your portfolio, you will want to project not only your own retirement needs and wants but also the amount that you would like to leave for your heirs. It can help to be a bit contrarian, because that often is an approach that makes money. The bond performance over the last thirty years is a case in point. I'm not saying you need to label yourself as a contrarian and doggedly swim against the current to be a success. I'm saying that you will be wise not to buy into the financial fashion of the moment.

That is the mark of empirical thinkers who look at the evidence and at the models and make independent decisions amid all the public chatter about what's hot and what's not. That is the mark of people with the confidence to cut their own path. All those talking heads and media commentators are dispensing advice for the masses. And it sells. You are an individual. Avoid the sales noise.

If you were a success in business, independent thinking was probably your nature anyway. You overcame the competition by discovering and marketing your own unique value. You took the road less traveled. Now, as you invest for retirement, my advice is this: keep doing that.

You are developing your own plan for a secure future that is everything you dreamed about. You need to follow your own course, not the course set up by someone who doesn't have a clue who you are, or what you need, or what you dream about, or what your family is like.

To be set for life is to be wealthy in ways that transcend the moment. You can be rich for a day, or for a season, but what you want is the kind of wealth that endures and outlasts you. That means preserving all that you have worked to attain and staying true to your life goals.

Unless you are driven from the start by a strong sense of purpose, you are at risk of doing the wrong things at the wrong time. You could succumb to the winds of fear or greed. Focusing on your vision helps to overcome that danger. You are not looking for a meteoric rise followed by a tumultuous fall. Instead, you are looking for steady progress toward a true wealth, and that calls for confidence to stay the course.

CHAPTER 8

PROTECTING
—Your—
LEGACY

As I was sitting in a restaurant with some clients, a husband and wife, a friend of theirs approached us with a smile of friendly greeting.

"So what are you all doing here together?" she asked after a few preliminaries. "You look like you're so deep in thought."

"We're talking about estate planning," the wife responded.

"Oh, I see," their friend simply said, but the look on her face revealed much more. She might as well have added: "Gag me!"

To many people, "estate" planning equates to planning for death. That is the connotation that they bring to the word. I understand, in a way. Even though it is arranging to leave money and other assets efficiently to the next generation, estate planning does involve a series of rather unpleasant decisions that minimize and eliminate.

The wife just as accurately could have announced that we were talking about legacy planning—in which case the connotation would have been one of enriching and building. People feel proud at the prospect of leaving a fruitful legacy to their children and other heirs. Good legacy planning also is a process of elimination in many ways. For one thing, it limits how much the government is included as a partner in the estate.

Legacy planning, however, does not begin with such particulars. It begins with a long ranging view of the decades ahead. That bigger picture perspective prevails and endures whether or not someone dies during the pursuit of it.

—— A MIND-SET OF ABUNDANCE ——

Whether you call it estate planning or legacy planning, it leads toward the same results. The difference is in approach. One is a mind-set of deficit, and the other is a mind-set of abundance.

Estate planning implies the nitty-gritty of wills and trusts, of finances and taxes, and how those will all come into play upon your death. When people talk of estate planning, they are generally in avoidance mode. They want to prevent something—namely, taxes. They want to minimize the damage.

By contrast, those who talk of legacy planning are trying to facilitate something. They deal with the same details, but the mind-set is inspirational. They envision a life of abundance and work to attain it. They imagine how they want their descendants to remember them someday, and they take the actions now that will make it happen. Along the way, they likewise tame the taxes, but they accomplish a whole lot more.

I once was involved in an estate meeting in which the family sat around a big table. At the head of the table was the multimillionaire patriarch, and with him were his wife, their two children, and a stepchild from his wife's previous marriage. His lawyer and accountant were prominently present as well. One of the children also had a lawyer, and one had brought along a therapist.

The patriarch did not seem all that enthusiastic about being there, but he wanted to get the job done. As the founder of the family fortune, he wanted to make sure that the company passed down to his own children while also providing something equitable for the stepchild. His wife was leaning toward protecting the stepchild's interests. All of these "children" were in their forties or fifties, and they had made their share of mistakes in life. Therefore, much of the focus was on protection of the assets.

In the end, a will was drawn up to slice the pie in the manner that had been most vehemently argued. The will tried to keep estate taxes to a minimum, but since they could not be altogether avoided the family decided to purchase a life insurance policy worth tens of millions of dollars. It would be owned by a trust. The policy payout would help to equalize the estate for the stepchild while also paying some of the estate taxes.

Although they agreed to the provisions, nobody was exactly happy as the family walked out of the room. The least happy of them all was the old man himself, the creator of the wealth. From his perspective, he was in the position of divvying up all that he had created. Everybody wanted something from him, beginning with the government which was ready to claim half. And the three children wanted the remainder, but for whatever reason felt entitled to more than their third.

These had been difficult decisions, and they were a matter of give and take. I, too, felt a knot in my stomach. I was in my late twenties or early thirties, and the other professionals and I had done our jobs and would be compensated fairly, but this had not been a fulfilling process for any of us. Everything was in place financially, but this process had not really strengthened the family. The patriarch had been running a successful company that was making lots of money and taking care of everybody nicely. Still, this had not been an exercise in planning for abundance. This had felt more like slicing up the pie.

Looking back, I can see that it might have been handled so differently. Instead of taxes driving the planning and the game ending up zero sum, the goal could have been growth in every area. Instead of buying insurance to pay estate taxes, the family could have leveraged that money to purchase the business back from a charity or charitable trust. The children who weren't involved in the business could have run the charity, and the wealth creator himself would have been focused on legacy, meaning and purpose, instead of on minimizing the tax damage. The real culprit was, and always is, lack of vision.

Legacy planning can be about living abundantly, now and through the generations, with the attitude of: "I'm going to continue to grow and control this wealth while I'm alive and beyond, so that it will have the impact that I envision."

When you have a vision, then all the unpleasantness of traditional estate planning can go away, and you can begin to take things into your own hands and grow the wealth to continue the good work for future generations. Your future is what legacy planning is all about. Estate planning is about the nuts and bolts of making it happen. It can be painful for a business owner to see family members squabbling over the details. It can be joyous to see them joining forces for the sake of prosperity.

—— WEALTH ON PURPOSE®

Once while I was attending a meeting of estate planners, a member of our profession stood up to tell us that the traditional approach he had taken with families for twenty years had left many of the heirs in worse shape than ever. A few, however, were thriving—and he proceeded to explain the difference.

Traditional estate planning, he pointed out, attempts to reduce the damage to assets using various tools and techniques, and then deals with the damage either with liquidity or life insurance in a trust. And that's it, other than deciding who gets what. Everybody gets their nice inheritance checks—but it comes to them without a sense of purpose.

And that, he concluded, ultimately had done harm in many of the families with which he had worked. Over the years, the money that heirs had received as result of their parents' estate planning had not helped them one bit. By contrast, he said, families who came to him with a clear vision seemed healthier over time as they grew to appreciate the wealth and use it wisely.

He clearly was on to something, and our profession has come to understand its importance: estate planning must focus first on the legacy and the purpose before giving any consideration to how the pie will be sliced.

In legacy planning, which we call "Wealth On Purpose® planning," you do not start out by minimizing the heavy toll of taxes, as traditional planning does. Instead you actually create more wealth that you control as you pursue your purpose. If you have a $100 million estate, you might leave $100 million to charity as well as $100 million to your children. The government gets nothing.

You might wonder how that could be possible, but America's wealthiest families have been doing this for generations, and the evidence of those charitable contributions is all around us. You see it in the many works done through the Ford Foundation, and the Bill & Melinda Gates Foundation, and many others. Those wealthy families, not the government, control that social capital.

After the future vision has been established, the details will fall into place. The tax savings will translate into capital for charity, in effect magnifying the power of the family's wealth. And then come all the specific considerations of estate planning: the setting up of wills and trusts, the drafting of essential documents and powers of attorney, and the logistics of protecting and distributing the assets.

It is not my purpose in this book to delve into those details, which can be found far and wide in libraries and on the Internet. My purpose is to emphasize how those details fit into your big picture and to focus on the philosophy that can bring you success.

A good estate attorney can help you to properly set up the specifics. Do not expect, however, that the attorney's first question will be: "So, what is your vision for the future?" Instead, you are likely to hear: "Here are all the bad things that happen, so let's talk about how to handle them." That is important work, of course. Those bad things certainly need to be addressed, but as a part of the process, and not the entire process.

You can easily get into the weeds with all those details, but people who have created a lot of wealth have done so with the help of good advisors on their team. As business people, they followed a vision, made sound decisions, took calculated risks, and delegated the tasks at hand to those with the expertise to manage them well. That is the approach for success at this stage of the game, too. Surround yourself with people who can provide you with the expertise and advice you need to make good decisions.

Those decisions can include cutting Uncle Sam out of the equation. You can choose who gets your money, and it need not be the government. You can do more to help the causes and institutions of your choice, all the while creating wealth to benefit your family. Your children and charity can be the main beneficiaries of your life's work.

Once you see that giving to charity can be in your own best interest, then the next question is whom do you want to help. Many people, considering that question for the first time, simply do not know. They have never really thought about it. They have yet to establish a vision. Sometimes spouses have never talked about the things that are most meaningful to them. It is high time they did.

—— SIMPLICITY OVER COMPLEXITY ——

Once you have been introduced to the possibilities, continue to do fact finding with your advisor to see how those possibilities might apply to you specifically. Based on what you have done so far and what you are currently doing, it's possible to assess what you could accomplish. Those are the steps that work. Seeing a vision and grasping the possibilities is the reason that people move forward. Otherwise, they often take the attitude of: "Let's not get so complicated." They somehow believe that they are avoiding complexity by not engaging in any purposeful legacy design.

In reality, when you are wealthy, life already is complicated. Most people want to simplify, and that is what this type of planning aims to do. It reaches for a simplicity of vision that gives meaning to the details. That is far different from simplicity that avoids the details. You are looking for the simplicity beyond the complexity.

Here is how former Supreme Court Justice Oliver Wendell Holmes, Jr. expressed the concept in his correspondence with British jurist Sir Frederick Pollock: "The only simplicity for which I would give a straw," Holmes wrote, "is that which is on the other side of the complex—not that which never has divined it."

Holmes was saying that we should not just keep it simple; instead, we should strive to attain simplicity. We can do that by first catching the vision, identifying the desired destination, and then setting out with a determination to get there. To insist on simplicity from the start will lead you to the slicing of the pie. To strive for a vision of simplicity will lead you to abundance.

I do have clients who have caught that vision. Their attitude is: "I have created $150 million, and I want my children to have enough—but not too much. I want to leave a lot to charity. In fact, I want to practice more philanthropy starting now and not wait until after I'm gone to do good in this world." Those are the people who understand what stewardship is all about, and I enjoy working with them as they tackle this responsibility and take control of their future.

I have often worked with families who are concerned about leaving too much money to the next generation, for fear that it could ultimately harm them. Affluent families often worry about spoiling the kids. I have had clients who, after doing some planning and developing their vision, have purposefully cut back on what the children will receive—perhaps $4 million each, rather than $10 million. They make a reasoned choice to provide less to their loved ones, and it is a decision wholly based on love. They know that it is the right thing to do.

I worked with a couple who were considering whether to leave several million dollars to each of their five children. They felt that two of them would do well with the inheritance, but the other three would simply stagnate and stop working. And one of those three, they told me, probably would whine that he was not getting enough—and he would feel that way no matter how much they left him.

What they were communicating, I realized, was that the two kids who were okay would still be okay no matter how much they inherited, but the other three, by their nature, would actually do worse with any amount. Ultimately, the couple did reduce the amount of money that they could have left to each of the children. They also decided to donate millions of dollars to charity over the ensuing years, helping a lot of people in their community while also realizing the tax benefits.

And I have observed, now that the couple have passed away, just how wise they were. One of the children now owns the family business and has been making some good choices, using the inheritance to leverage his success. It was sufficient to motivate him to greater heights. Meanwhile, the couple bestowed an enduring legacy on their community. They engaged in some brilliant thinking. In their vision, they found the simplicity beyond the complexity.

— WHEN RIGHTS GO WRONG

Parents tend to know which of their children will carry forth the vision and which will not. They want to put their money where it will do the most

good, but at the same time they do not want to cause a war among siblings.

This calls for some creative and delicate decision-making. Family issues often come to the fore. Spouses often disagree when issues surface that have gone unspoken for many years. Perhaps they recognized the problem but did not want to set off a powder keg.

These decisions can be particularly difficult in blended families, although couples do often disagree over the distribution of assets to the children that they had together. Perhaps a son is involved in the business, but the daughter is not. Dad wants to divide the resources equitably. Mom wants to divide the resources equally. The words do not mean the same thing.

The biblical account of Jacob and Esau amounts to a lesson on estate planning—or rather, how not to do estate planning. It's a story of deception and contention between siblings and spouses over a major inheritance.

Jacob and Esau were the twin sons of Isaac and Rebekah. The twins' grandparents were Abraham and Sarah, to whom God had promised a family that one day would be as numerous as the stars. Isaac's favorite son was Esau, who was born with thick hair and grew up even hairier, becoming an adventurous hunter. Rebekah's favorite son was Jacob, who was smooth-skinned and soft-spoken, and who stayed at home and kept her company.

Esau had been the first of the twins to be born, and therefore it was his birthright to inherit his father's lands and lead the family. One day Esau came home from hunting, tired and famished, and asked his brother for some of the stew he was making. Jacob offered him some, but only if Esau would promise to give him his inheritance in return. Esau agreed.

When Jacob told his mother about this development, Rebekah explained that it was not so simple and that the decision was Isaac's to make. She knew that Isaac still would give that special blessing to Esau, regardless of any promise over a bowl of soup.

Years later, when Isaac was very old, he called for Esau and told him to prepare to get his blessing. Esau went off to hunt for some fresh meat for the occasion. Rebekah, hearing this, urged Jacob to slip into his father's tent and get the blessing while Esau was away. His father was nearly blind, she told him, and would not know the difference. She wrapped her son's arms and neck in goatskins so Isaac would not feel his smooth skin if he touched him. The ruse worked. Jacob received his father's blessing—and got the full inheritance.

When Esau returned from the hunt, Isaac realized to his dismay that he had been tricked and explained what had happened. Nothing could be done now to turn this around, he said, his heart breaking. The blessing could not be taken back. What was done was done.

I have seen families similarly maneuver for inheritance rights, particularly when there is a business in play. Sometimes it feels like a cold war. Wealthy families, with more tools at their disposal, sometimes use them for deceptive power plays, and their lawyers and accountants and advisors can get caught up in that minefield. Siblings who consider their inheritance to be some God-given right can end up feeling cheated and alienated from one another, or from their parents. The parents know their children's strengths and weaknesses, and sometimes, like Isaac and Rebekah, they play favorites.

The contention can indeed become intense—but the good news is that it need not be that way. With thoughtful planning and a clear vision, everyone can come out ahead. Open and honest communication is the key. Ideally, family members are talking all along about how together they will strive for success and how they will support one another along the way. With the guidance of a professional advisor who understands the dynamics involved, the future can be bright for all.

CONCLUSION:

— The Better Path —

In virtually every chapter, I have emphasized the importance of vision and purpose. That is because untold riches can be lost when these are lacking. It can cost you a fortune, not only in money but in richness of life as well. It leads to a separation not only from your wealth but from people.

When you do have a vision, however, you can transform a costly liability into a fruitful investment. The vision gives birth to that transformation. No longer is your focus on how much you might lose. You now focus on the abundance you could gain. When you get your castle, you may find that it still needs a moat, but there never would have been a castle unless you had dreamed it.

The mind-set of abundance doesn't mean you do not play defense. It means that you know that ultimately it will be your offense that scores the touchdown. You will still be taking care of the details and planning for them. Your defense will be there to block the threats, while your offense makes the pass and runs the ball. That's how you will get the points on the board. An effective offense requires a good game plan—or, you might say, a powerful vision for how you will score.

I have had the most success with clients when I have insisted that the vision come before the details, or we would not be working together. Recently I was working with several members of a family that was setting up a charitable foundation. They could not agree on a strategy. Some pushed for a simplistic approach that would have resulted in less money both for the charities and for themselves. I considered telling them that the direction they were going was so wrong that they were risking their relationship with me, but I realized that what they truly needed to do was to focus on their ultimate aim. I asked them to get together and write a memo stating clearly what they were trying to achieve, and what was important to them and what was not. That clarity made all the difference. They chose the better path.

The very structure of this book reflects the emphasis I place on vision first. The opening section explores the philosophy upon which the ensuing sections and chapters are predicated. We have covered a lot of ground in our discussions of wealth management and taxation and transition planning and much more, but it has all come back to the primacy of purpose. Where are you in life? Where are you going? What's it all about? Those are the questions that every day I remind my clients to keep foremost in their thoughts as we delve into the details and plan their ideal futures.

My firm serves successful entrepreneurs and business leaders in the area of wealth design; more specifically, Business Wealth Design™. As such, it is our place to design and then deliver plans and programs that help build wealth for business people. If you would like information on our services or simply have questions after reading this book, the team would love to hear from you: www.lwmg.com.

ABOUT
— *The* —
AUTHOR

Carlos H. Lowenberg, Jr.,ChFC®
Founder and CEO

Carlos H. Lowenberg, Jr., ChFC®, has over twenty years of experience in the financial services industry. He is the founder and CEO of a successful boutique business management and financial services firm in Austin, Texas, serving entrepreneurial-minded individuals.

His firm helps clients add value to their businesses through Business Transition Planning, Key Person Reward and Retention Strategies and Wealth Preservation. In addition, Mr. Lowenberg has extensive knowledge, insight, and experience in all aspects of Family Wealth Counseling, Charitable Estate Planning, and Wealth Transfer Planning. He also is the creator of the Wealth on Purpose® system and the Social Capital Opportunity™ approach to legacy and estate planning.

Mr. Lowenberg has often been the featured speaker at seminars and conferences in the financial services industry and has advised law firms and accounting firms in charitable and estate planning. He has been a frequent guest on CNBC's *Power Lunch* and has been interviewed by *Business Week* as well. His writings have been published in numerous places including Forbes.com, *Investment News, Austin Business Journal, Austin American Statesman,* MarketWatch.com, MSN Money, *SmartMoney* and many more. Mr. Lowenberg's insights on "Making Your Charitable Donations Count— Five Tips in Choosing the Right Charity," were featured on MarketWatch.

com. He is also a contributor to the book entitled *Family Wealth Counseling—Getting to the Heart of the Matter* by Mr. E.G. "Jay" Link, one of the foremost experts on issues and strategies relating to charitable planning techniques for wealthy families.

Mr. Lowenberg is a member of a number of industry organizations, including: the Association for Advanced Life Underwriters (AALU), the National Association of Insurance Financial Advisors (NAIFA) and The International Forum. Carlos is also Chairman of the Board of City School Austin and a member of the board of the Austin Lyric Opera.

Carlos and his family reside in Austin, Texas.

Printed in the USA
CPSIA information can be obtained
at www.ICGtesting.com
JSHW012012140824
68134JS00023B/2371